A Cry from the Earth

Books edited by John Bierhorst

The Fire Plume / *Legends of the American Indians*

The Ring in the Prairie / *A Shawnee Legend*

In the Trail of the Wind / *American Indian Poems and Ritual Orations*

Songs of the Chippewa

Four Masterworks of American Indian Literature / *Quetzalcoatl, The Ritual of Condolence, Cuceb, The Night Chant*

The Red Swan / *Myths and Tales of the American Indians*

Black Rainbow / *Legends of the Incas and Myths of Ancient Peru*

The Girl Who Married a Ghost and Other Tales from the North American Indian

A CRY FROM THE EARTH

Music of the North American Indians

by John Bierhorst

Ancient City Press

SANTA FE / NEW MEXICO

International Standard Book Number: 0-941270-53-X paperback

Library of Congress Cataloging in Publication Data

Bierhorst, John.
A cry from the earth : music of the
North American Indians / by John Bierhorst.
p.   cm.
Originally published: New York : Four Winds Press, 1979.
Includes bibliographical references and index.
Summary: An overview of American Indian music and dance which
includes a discussion of their instruments, the structure
of their music, and the uses of music in Indian life.
ISBN 0-941270-53-X
1. Indians of North America — Music — History and criticism —
[1. Indians of North America — Music.] I. Title.
[ML3557.B53   1992]
91-47634   781.62'97 — dc20   CIP MN AC

Book and cover design by Jane Byers Bierhorst
First Ancient City Press Printing, 1992
10 9 8 7 6 5 4 3 2

Frontispiece / "Singing Deeds of Valor" (Teton Sioux),
Edward S. Curtis, *The North American Indian*,
vol. 3, p. 82. Courtesy of Vassar College.
Cover photograph / *Peyote Drummer* by Edward S. Curtis, 1927.
Plate number 687. Courtesy of the Laboratory of
Anthropology of the Museum of New Mexico.

Foreword

Music is an essential part of Indian life. It is used in connection with almost every activity from baby-sitting to mourning for the dead. It helps control the weather, it is used in storytelling, it serves as a greeting, and it expresses thanks. One purpose of this book is to demonstrate these different uses and to show how music plays an important role not only in everyday life but on occasions of great joy or sadness and in times of danger.

A second purpose is to show the wide variety in Indian music. Songs of the Northwest Coast, for example, are entirely different from songs used by the people of the Great Basin. In this book at least one song, and in most cases two or more songs, are presented from each major region. These songs illustrate the concept of "musical areas" developed by such well-known investigators as George Herzog, Helen Roberts, and Bruno Nettl.

But it has not been considered sufficient to present musical examples that are merely representative. In preparing this book thousands of songs have been either listened to or studied in transcription in order to find those examples that demonstrate the melodic and rhythmic ingenuity of Indian musical art at its best. These are songs that can be appreciated—and sung—by Indians and non-Indians alike.

The present collection has two other unusual features: it spans the entire historical period for which musical examples are available (from the late eighteenth century to the mid-twentieth), and it represents the work of virtually every important collector, including not only such famous names as Frances Densmore, Willard Rhodes, George Herzog, and Marius Barbeau, but rare items from the collections of Washington Matthews, Alice Fletcher, Edward S. Curtis, Natalie Curtis, James Mooney, J.P. Harrington, Frank Speck, Wallace Chafe, Frederica de Laguna, and others.

The original native performances of most of these

songs can be heard on the record album carrying the same title, *A Cry from the Earth* (3777 Folkways Cassette Series, available from the Smithsonian Institution). The book and the album have been planned so that they may be used together. Yet each is complete in itself, and each may be used independently.

This project could not have been carried through without the good will and expertise of numerous individuals and institutions. I thank them all. In particular, I thank the Interlibrary Loan Division of the Mid-Hudson Libraries, Poughkeepsie, New York, for conveying research materials; the Archive of Folk Song (Library of Congress), the Archives of Traditional Music (Indiana University), and National Museums of Canada for supplying duplicate tapes and related information; and Willard Rhodes, Professor Emeritus, Columbia University, for reading the manuscript.

J.B.

West Shokan, N.Y.
July, 1978

Contents

A Cry from the Earth

A Different Kind of Music

A lone horseman is crossing the desert late at night. Afraid of the dark, he begins to sing. As the music flows out from his body, filling the night air around him, it creates an invisible zone of protection. No evil spirit can penetrate within hearing range of the song. The rider now has what he calls a "cover."

It is the Navajo, who live in the deserts of northern Arizona and New Mexico, who protect themselves under the "cover" of a song. But the idea that music has supernatural power is shared by Indians throughout North America. Music is used to cure disease, to bring rain, to win a lover, or to defeat an enemy. If you can sing, you have the ability to influence the world around you.

Today this feeling is strongest among older Indians and among those tribes that have been able to preserve their traditional ways. Many younger Indians sing mainly for pleasure or to express their pride in being Indian, just as when people in England sing "God Save the Queen" they are saying, in effect, that they are proud to be English.

In the old days, too, Indians often sang for pleasure. In the Southwest, for example, Indian women would sing while grinding corn. Yet the words to these corn-grinding songs were prayers for rain. A girl might be heard crooning to her baby brother, but what she would really be doing would be putting forth sleep magic. There were very few songs that did not have some definite purpose, and it is this purposefulness, more than anything else, that distinguishes Indian music from the music of modern Europe or America.

Dancing to restore an eclipsed
moon, Kwakiutl.

How Songs Are Made

In a traditional Indian community, songs are so important that no one can afford to be without them. In many tribes songs are regarded as personal property. You may not sing someone else's song unless you buy it from him—assuming he is willing to sell it. Song priests and medicine men have elaborate chants that they learn from their teachers. But ordinary people are often forced to make up their own songs. How do they do it?

Creativity either comes or it doesn't. It cannot be willed. Realizing this, Indian song makers sometimes say that their inspiration comes from an animal helper speaking to them in a vision or dream. A more modern idea is that creativity flows from an inner, or deep, part of the brain beyond our conscious control. When we dream, it is this inner part of the mind that speaks to us and makes strange pictures. Sometimes it speaks in music.

Many Indian singers do indeed wait for dreams to bring them new songs. Among the Ute Indians of the Great Basin, people are said to "hear" songs in their sleep and wake up singing them. The old-time Ute recognized no other method of composition.

Just as in non-Indian societies, some individuals are less gifted than others. In fact it is always a problem when boys come of age and are expected to compose the vision songs that will be their power when they are men. Not every boy is a natural musician. With repeated coaching, however, a young man learns what melodies and what words are acceptable. He goes off and tries to dream. Finally he comes back with a song that will serve the purpose even if it is little more than an imitation of something he has heard from his master.

But not all songs are received in dreams. Many are deliberately composed. In the case of songs used in sacred ceremonies the source is kept secret, and it is said that these songs were given by a mythic hero in the ancient days or that they were carried up by the first people when they emerged from the earth.

Speech Rhythm and Body Rhythm

Many people think music has to have a beat, a regular, foot-tapping kind of body rhythm that you can dance to. Even though this body rhythm may be distorted or obscured, it must always be there. The poet Ezra Pound has said that poetry comes from music, and music comes from dance. In other words all poetry and music must have an underlying dancelike rhythm.

But this is not necessarily true. Birds do not dance when they sing, nor do we dance or tap our feet when we talk. And yet the singing of birds, like the speech of humans, does indeed have a rhythm. When foreigners attempt to speak English they sometimes accent the wrong syllables or pronounce certain syllables a little too quickly or a little too slowly. It is easy to tell that they have the wrong "speech rhythm."

Like most other rhythms that occur in nature, speech rhythm cannot be reduced to a regular oompah, oompah, oompah. And neither can many Indian songs. These songs are really a form of musical speech. That's why, when we write them in modern notation, we sometimes have to make up a different time signature for every measure. Notice the Hopi "Sleep Song" on page 33 or the Pima "Flute Song" on page 81. Putting these songs into notation is like putting them into a straitjacket.

The same is true, to a much lesser degree, with the music of a composer like Chopin. A pianist who plays these melodies with strict body rhythm is said to have no talent. Chopin must be played with a somewhat free rhythm that imitates speech.

There is reason to suppose that when humans first began to sing, thousands of years ago, they sang in speech rhythm. Only much later did people learn to force their music into the regular patterns of body rhythm. But it is interesting to note that in the past two hundred years European music—or as we say, Western music—has moved steadily back toward speech.

Most people, of course, are not willing to go much farther in this direction than Chopin, whose melodies are still accompanied by a more or less regular body rhythm.

The Ball Play dance, Choctaw,
painted by George Catlin
in the 1830s.

Few people have even heard of the important art-music composers of our own time, composers like Anton Webern and Karlheinz Stockhausen, whose rhythms are like the speech of birds or like the sound of raindrops hitting the surface of a pond. Here where Western music ends, Indian music begins.

Not all Indian songs obey the laws of speech rhythm, however. Some songs show definite signs of body rhythm, and many others have already arrived. The rhythm is perfectly regular. Notice the Kwakiutl cradle song on page 36. We may say, then, that Indian music is *in the process* of emerging from nature.

Another feature of Indian music should perhaps be mentioned in this connection. Just as in the "music" of birds, Indian music does not always keep to the fixed tones that can be played on the piano. Some notes are actually quarter tones—in between the halftones on the piano. And here and there a note may be made up of several tones, like a syllable of ordinary speech. Modern American jazz singers sometimes use speech tones to achieve a talking effect, but if you go out and buy the sheet music, you won't find any indication of it on the printed page. Similarly there has been no attempt in this book to mark quarter tones or speech tones.

Singing in the Throat

When you hear people singing "America the Beautiful" or "The Star-Spangled Banner," most of them are singing with a completely open throat. Try it. Sing a few bars of any familiar song. Sing loud enough and you will feel the vibration in the roof of your mouth. Make sure your throat is perfectly relaxed and fully open. Voice teachers call this "singing up," or "singing in the head." In Western music this kind of singing is much desired.

But most Indians sing down in the throat. To get the right feeling pretend that you are sobbing, that you are literally choked up with emotion. You will feel the catch in your throat. Take one of your sobs and let the sound keep coming. Now turn that sound into a song, any famil-

Singing with a tight throat,
Arikara medicine ceremony.

iar song. The music will be coming from that place in your throat where you felt the catch. No matter how loud you sing, you will not feel the vibration in the roof of your mouth. You will feel it only in your throat.

When you sing this way the tone is a little heavier, a little darker than when you sing with a fully relaxed,

open throat. This is a good way to sing when you try almost any Indian song.

Now try singing not only "in the throat" but with an extremely tight throat, so tight that your lungs have to push hard in order to force air through the tiny opening that is left. The tone will be hard and vibrant. If you sing low it may sound gravelly. If you sing high it may whine. You will find that even your face muscles are now very tense. This is the way Indian men, not women, sing in the Plains area and around the western Great Lakes.

In addition they let the tone come out with a rapid or slow pulsing, producing with the voice a kind of drum-beat effect on long notes. No other people in the world are quite able to do this. This kind of singing is uniquely Indian. Needless to say, it is very difficult. Young Sioux and Chippewa men practice endlessly before they achieve the proper sound.

Pueblo men, when they sing sacred music, also keep a very tense throat. In the Eastern Woodlands and in the Far West the throat is only slightly tense. And in the

Gray Eyes and Chee singing
Navajo love songs.

Great Basin and in parts of California, Indians sing with a quite relaxed throat. It is even possible that these people may sometimes "sing up," with the sound vibrating in the mouth. The question is difficult to discuss because no one has ever made a thorough study of it.

It is interesting that Indian women rarely, if ever, sing with a tense throat. To do so would be considered unfeminine. Such a restriction seems odd when we think of the exaggerated vocal displays permitted both male and female singers in such fields as jazz and rock, or indeed any area of modern music. Clearly, a woman who is not Indian should feel no more inhibition than a man in attempting the "masculine" singing style.

A Cry from the Earth

No one really knows how music originated. Some people think it comes from speech. It has already been pointed out that many Indian songs have speech rhythm. Perhaps melody also comes from speech. Among the

Navajo this can actually be demonstrated.

The Navajo language, like Chinese, is what we call a tone language. The meaning of a word depends upon whether you say it high or say it low. When these words find their way into a song they tend to keep their high or low tone, thus creating melody of themselves. In most other languages, of course, this effect cannot be observed.

Another idea about the origin of music is that melody appears spontaneously in the voice of a person who is deeply moved or upset. If, as you are speaking, you begin to laugh or cry, your voice does become somewhat melodious. It was the British philosopher Herbert Spencer who suggested that music originated in this way. Nowadays Spencer's theory is not much talked about, yet there is evidence to show that Indians would agree with him.

From tribes all over North America come reports of songs that begin or end in weeping. In some cases people actually cry when they sing. Of course crying can express joy as well as sorrow. Take a moment now to look at two of the most beautiful songs in this book. One is a laughing song (page 38), the other a weeping song (page

Isleta boy with hand drum.

11

86). In these songs you can hear the jerky peals of laughter and the convulsive sobs.

The Navajo say that in the ancient days a song was born from the tears of the earth mother. Her son, who was to become one of the great heroes of the Navajo, had grown up and had left her. In her loneliness she began to cry. As she cried, her weeping became music.

From Out of the Fire

When the world was new and the first people had been formed out of clay, a great serpent came up from the ocean. The people made a circle of brushwood and the serpent coiled his body inside it. Then the people set the brushwood on fire. When the fire got hot, the serpent exploded and scattered. Inside his body were all languages, all customs, and all songs. As a result of the fire these were strewn across the land. This is why people today speak different languages and sing different kinds of songs.

Such stories—like this one from the Diegueño of southern California—account for a fact that non-Indians often fail to appreciate. Many people have the idea that all Indian songs sound alike. Yet nothing could be farther from the truth.

The study of primitive music, including Indian music, is called *ethnomusicology*. Over the past fifty years ethnomusicologists, after listening repeatedly to different kinds of Indian songs, have learned to divide them into groups corresponding to geographical areas. Although sometimes the music of one group spills over into another area, each has its own special kind of singing, different from all others.

Eskimo Music

In opera the singing that comes between the arias, or songs, is known as recitative. This kind of singing is not very melodious. Yet the words that go with it are usually

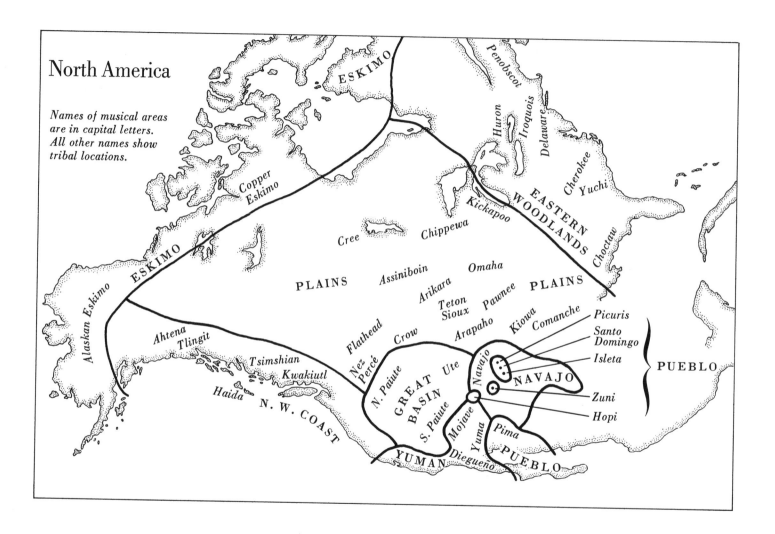

North America

Names of musical areas
are in capital letters.
All other names show
tribal locations.

ESKIMO

Copper
Eskimo

Penobscot

ESKIMO

Huron

Iroquois

Delaware

Cherokee

Yuchi

EASTERN WOODLANDS

Kickapoo

Cree

Chippewa

Choctaw

Alaskan Eskimo

Assiniboin

Omaha

PLAINS

Arikara

Teton
Sioux

Pawnee

PLAINS

Ahtena
Tlingit

Flathead

Crow

Arapaho

Kiowa

Comanche

Picuris

Santo
Domingo

Tsimshian

Kwakiutl

Nez
Percé

N. Paiute

GREAT
BASIN

Ute

Navajo

Isleta

Haida

N. W. COAST

S. Paiute

NAVAJO

Zuni

Hopi

PUEBLO

Mojave

Yuma

Pima

YUMAN

Diegueño

PUEBLO

14

more interesting than the words to the arias. It is the recitative that tells the story.

Most Eskimo songs can be classed as recitative. Like other native American songs they use speech rhythm, but to such an extent that the singing begins to sound very much like talking itself. In some Eskimo communities singing actually takes the place of a newspaper. People get together and sing the latest gossip or the latest news. If two men have an argument they sometimes settle the dispute musically, singing insults at each other and allowing the audience to pick the winner. Another popular kind of song is the weather incantation, a song in which the singer tries to make the wind subside or the sun come out by talking to himself or to his guardian spirit. Any of these songs may be accompanied by a large, flat, tambourine-like drum, the only instrument Eskimos use.

The little song on page 51 is a typical short weather incantation. Its melody may not be very interesting, but it has the most intriguing words of any song in this book.

Music of the Northwest Coast

Most songs, including most Indian songs, keep to the regular notes we call *do, re, mi, fa, sol, la, ti, do*. Music of this type is called diatonic, a word that comes from the Greek and means something like "regular tones." Of course, many Indian and Eskimo songs use just a few of these tones, for example the Eskimo song on page 51, which has only *do, mi, fa,* and *la*. Even this little song can be called diatonic.

But some songs have extra, or "foreign," notes added in. These notes are the halftones that come betweeen *do* and *re, re* and *mi, fa* and *sol, sol* and *la,* and *la* and *ti*. We sometimes call such halftones "accidentals" (sharps, flats, or naturals that are written after the key signature at the beginning of the line). Any song that makes use of them is said to be chromatic, another Greek word, meaning "colorful."

The Kwakiutl, Tlingit, Tsimshian, and other tribes living along the Northwest Coast have music that is definitely "colorful." It cannot get along without extra

Musicians at a Tlingit potlatch, Sitka, Alaska.

ter. It comes as no surprise, therefore, that the people of the Northwest Coast have exceptionally beautiful songs for the dead. See the Tsimshian and Tlingit mourning songs on pages 86 and 89.

These people have another kind of music, however, that is not necessarily chromatic. In this music, members of a chorus take different parts. The Tlingit "Greeting Song," given on page 17, is a good example. In addition to the two parts that are written, there may sometimes be a third part, three or four halftones higher than the top line. And people who have very high or very low voices sing an octave higher or lower. When you hear a chorus singing like this, it has a wonderful, organlike sound, as though a gigantic musical top were spinning or someone were playing chords on a huge harmonica.

The "Greeting Song," sung in the eighteenth century, is one of the first Indian songs ever written down. Today Tlingit choruses still perform music very much like it. But singing in parts is not common, even along the Northwest Coast. In other areas it is extremely rare or nonexistent. In fact one of the main characteristics of Indian music is that it does not use part singing.

sharps and flats. Take a look at the Kwakiutl cradle song (page 36) and the Tsimshian "Lullaby for a Girl" (page 38). These chromatic songs have an almost eerie quality, even though the "Lullaby for a Girl" is filled with laugh-

Greeting Song

TLINGIT

Anonymous, 1786

In general, the songs of the Northwest Coast are longer and more involved than the songs of other areas. Nevertheless, these songs often use recitative, as in Eskimo music, and they are often accompanied by the Eskimo drum. This shows the relationship between Eskimos and their Northwest Coast neighbors. Both peoples are believed to have migrated from Asia not too many thousands of years ago.

The Yuman Style

Indians of southern California and western Arizona like to string their songs together in a musical program that sometimes lasts all night and may include dancing. The most famous of these song-cycles is the Deer Dance. Typically, it tells the story of a journey, in this case the journey of a deer. Another is the Wildcat Dance, which may also tell the story of an animal journey, but we do not have enough information about it to be sure.

In the song from the Wildcat Dance on page 57 you will discover two of the most important features of Yuman music. One is the triplet rhythm that occurs on the first and fourth beats of the first measure, and the other is the so-called rise, a slightly higher part in the middle of the song. During the rise the rattle accompaniment becomes a rapid tremolo.

Yuman songs, though they are probably sung in the throat, are sung with almost no vocal tension. The sound is very much as in European or modern American singing.

Navajo Music

Music is so important—so sacred—to the Navajo that rarely would you be able to hear casual singing around an old-style Navajo homestead. The most important singing of all takes place in the nine-day chants, or "sings," held for the purpose of curing disease. Everyone who wants to feel better comes and listens.

To the Navajo this music is especially beautiful because it brings healing. But people who are not Navajo have difficulty understanding it, because, to tell the truth, Navajo music is not very melodious. Nor does it have to be. The reason, perhaps, is that the Navajo use tones when they speak (see page 11). Therefore even a very simple melody has an extra richness for Navajo listeners. In their language, tones are like words.

Many Navajo songs sound a little like bugle calls, not in the way they are sung but because of the notes they use. Try the "Dove Song" on page 53 and you will get the idea.

Navajo songs are sung with a moderate amount of tension in the throat. A Navajo singer, when he is young, swallows a piece of turquoise so that his voice will always be beautiful.

Songs of the Great Basin

The native people of Utah and Nevada sing songs that are simple, yet quite melodious. One of the most important tribes in this area is the Paiute, who nearly a hundred years ago started a new religion, the Ghost Dance, which spread to many other tribes in the western United States. All these tribes began to sing Ghost Dance songs, and the songs were always in the Paiute, or Great Basin, style. You will find examples on pages 93–94.

Great Basin songs often sound a little like English nursery songs. Notice the Cherokee lullaby on page 34. The Cherokee live far from Nevada and Utah, and it may be just a coincidence that this lullaby sounds like a Great Basin song. It has been observed, however, that certain Indian lullabies and almost all Indian storytelling songs either come from the Great Basin or are left over from a long-ago musical style that now flourishes mainly among the Paiute and their neighbors.

Great Basin songs are sung with an almost fully relaxed throat, as in Yuman singing.

The Plains Style

This is perhaps the most important Indian style and one of the great musical styles of the world. The melodies

Old-style formality is relaxed
at a modern Navajo Squaw Dance.

are bold and majestic, starting high up and driving downward to a final note perhaps an octave and a half lower than the starting point. All you have to do is sing a few notes of a typical Plains song and people immediately recognize it as being Indian. This is the style that is always imitated by non-Indians when they need "Indian" sound effects. What must not be lacking are (1) intervals of three halftones, called "minor thirds," for example the skip from C down to A, (2) mixed with other small intervals in a generally descending line, (3) marked by frequent sixteenth-note accentuations and (4) insistent repetitions of one important note, called the "keynote," especially at the end of the piece. All four features may be observed in the song "Clear the Way," page 73, and even more so in the modern love song on page 21.

The influence of the Plains style can be felt in Pueblo music and, to a lesser extent, in the music of the Eastern Woodlands. There are even traces of it along the Northwest Coast. Nowadays when Indians get together, no matter what tribe they happen to belong to, they often sing Plains songs, or songs that are obviously derived from this style, thus giving rise to a somewhat new kind of singing (often with English words) known as pan-Indian.

The above-mentioned love song is a convenient example of the pan-Indian style. Few listeners will fail to recognize it as Indian. The effect is exaggerated by an abundance of "minor thirds" (see explanation above). But the lyrics express modern, not traditional, ideas. And the bold melody may have been adapted from an old Sioux ceremonial song, perhaps even a war song. In a concession to modern taste the singer performs the first nine notes an octave lower than traditional style would dictate.

It is indeed difficult for the average voice to encompass the range required in Plains songs. If need be, there is no harm in transposing (singing in a different key).

Pueblo Music

Pueblo music is a mixture of different styles, especially Plains, but also Great Basin and even Yuman. What makes this music distinctive is that it has taken a variety of musical ideas and put them into songs that are in some ways even more complicated than the songs of the Northwest Coast.

Modern Love Song

PAN-INDIAN

Sung by Leah K. Hicks, 1941

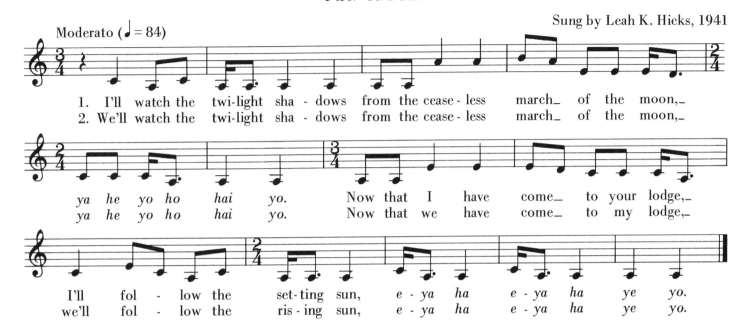

Moderato (♩ = 84)

1. I'll watch the twi-light sha - dows from the cease - less march of the moon,
2. We'll watch the twi-light sha - dows from the cease - less march of the moon,

ya he yo ho hai yo. Now that I have come to your lodge,
ya he yo ho hai yo. Now that we have come to my lodge,

I'll fol - low the set-ting sun, e - ya ha e - ya ha ye yo.
we'll fol - low the ris-ing sun, e - ya ha e - ya ha ye yo.

Take a look at the Hopi "Sleep Song" on page 33. This little piece, though much shorter than most Pueblo songs, has almost all the features a Pueblo song ought to have. Notice that it is made up of three melodic themes. The first three measures give one theme, the next two measures give a second, and the rest of the song gives yet a third. This kind of complexity is especially typical of the more westerly pueblos.

Notice also that the fifth measure is faster. A sudden change in speed is typical of Pueblo music. Another typical feature is the long note near the end of each of the first three measures. This is called "lengthening."

Music of the Eastern Woodlands

The Penobscot song on page 67 comes from the Maine woods, yet it sounds amazingly like a Scandinavian folk song—in that it uses the first five notes of the minor scale, often hesitating on the second, resulting in a rather tender plaintiveness. Is it possible that the Vikings brought their music with them, and left it here, when they visited the New World a thousand years ago? Probably not. More than likely this is just one of those strange coincidences that leads people to jump to conclusions.

Now look at the Choctaw song on page 68. Its bouncy rhythm sounds African. Is it possible that black Africans who were brought to the southern United States as slaves influenced Indian music? Some people think so. But this too may be just a coincidence.

The "Scandinavian" melodies are not found outside

A modern Iroquois performance
with Plains costumes near
Brantford, Ontario.

New England. But among the Iroquois of New York we do find the "African" ones. In this case no one would question that the melodies are, after all, purely Indian.

In the Iroquois Drum Dance song on page 59, a solo singer is answered by a chorus. It is as though a question were asked by the soloist and the answer given by the chorus. This kind of singing is called "antiphonal," and it is also found in African music—and in Navajo music. See page 64. But in North America it is especially typical of the Eastern Woodlands.

Notice also that the Drum Dance song has a swinging, or bouncy, rhythm. This kind of rhythm is called "syncopated." It too is typical of the Eastern Woodlands. The Delaware "Peyote Song" (page 97) is one of the swingingest songs in this book, yet it cannot be said for sure that this is due to Eastern Woodlands influence only. Many Peyote songs show the influence of the Yuman style, in which syncopated effects are not uncommon.

Because certain eastern tribes were exterminated by white settlers in colonial times, it is not possible for us to know what their music sounded like. Nevertheless, it seems fair to say that the question-and-answer style and the swinging rhythm were widespread in eastern North America long before the arrival of Columbus.

Propping Up the Songs

Except for the native flute, musical instruments that can be used to play a melody are rare among North American Indians. There isn't much solo instrumental music and there are no orchestras at all. The most common instruments, drums and rattles, are used primarily to accompany singing. Indians believe that these instruments "help" the singers. Among the Iroquois it is said that the instruments "prop up" the songs.

Drums

Drums are the most important and widespread of all Indian instruments. Although other tribes do not have this custom, the Santo Domingo Indians of New Mexico treat drums as persons—just as in Africa—and give each drum its own name.

The most popular drum is the hand drum, which sometimes looks like a tambourine and, like the tambourine, is made by stretching a piece of animal skin over a narrow, very thin plank of wood bent into a circular frame. Illustrations are on pages 51 and 88.

Large drums are made by hollowing out a section of log, one to three feet long, and stretching hide over one or both ends. These drums usually rest on the ground and may be played by several people at once. In the Plains area, people sometimes hang large drums from stakes. Underneath they dig a shallow pit, which gives the drum a fuller sound. It is said that the large drum used by the Chippewa can be heard ten miles away.

Water drums are made by stretching a piece of skin over a clay pot, an iron kettle, or a section cut from a small log hollowed out so that one end remains closed. Before the skin is stretched, the drum is partly filled with water to give it a more pleasing tone. The water drum is used to accompany various songs, including Peyote songs. It is illustrated on pages 58 and 96.

A most unusual drum is the wooden-box drum made by the Northwest Coast Indians. Another is the California and Northwest Coast "foot drum," a large plank laid over a pit, played by stomping. The Delaware Indians used to beat a rolled up deerskin. In the Southwest baskets are used. Some singers nowadays use a modern snare drum or bass drum. If you have no drum at all, you may simply slap your body, as Eskimo singers often do.

The Art of Drumming

If you do have a drum, you must not beat it with your bare hands. Indian drums, except in rare cases, are played

Chippewa instruments. *Left to right* | birchbark rolls inscribed with pictographs representing songs, hand-drum-shaped rattle with beating stick, large ceremonial drum with curved stick, small hand-drum-shaped rattle with long beating stick, three rattles made of sewn hide.

with a stick, often with a piece of cloth or hide wrapped around the end.

Drum notation is given with several of the songs in this book. In most of these songs the drumbeat seems to fit in with the rhythm of the melody. But many other songs are accompanied by a beat that is very definitely in a different rhythm—for example, the middle part of the lullaby given on page 38. How can this be? If you try to tap your foot in one rhythm, while singing in a different (regular) rhythm, you will find that you simply can't do it. But now try reciting your name and address while tapping your hand in any rhythm you wish. This is easy. There is no problem when you combine speech rhythm with body rhythm.

We do not know how fast the drumbeat was that accompanied the song "To Quiet a Raging Storm," page 51. For some reason the machine that recorded this song was unable to pick up the drum. Yet because the song is in speech rhythm, it could have been sung to a drumbeat either faster or slower than the "beat" of the song itself. As an experiment try singing this song in a moderate tempo. Tap your hand very rapidly at about the speed of an electric typewriter, or as fast as you can. Now slow the tapping to about the speed of a ticking clock. Finally, choose any speed you like that gives the song a pleasing textural background. In order to achieve this double performance you must free yourself from the mistaken idea that this song is in regular meter. Think of it as pure speech.

Music like this, in which two or more parts, though heard together, have no connection with each other, is typical of the Indian way of thinking. There are even Indian dances in which the steps are executed in a rhythm entirely independent of the accompanying song. Indian myth makers do the same kind of thing. When they tell stories about Coyote, they have him lighting a fire, shooting a bow, and getting married—things only a human could do. Is Coyote an animal or a man? The answer is that he is both things at once.

By insisting that everything be perfectly consistent, non-Indians have cut themselves off from the double vision that gives Indian art, poetry, and music its special flavor.

Rattles

American Indian rattles are of three basic types. The first is a container in which pebbles or other small objects are shaken. Gourds are often used in this manner. A hide pouch, a clay pot, or even a turtle shell may do as well.

The second type of rattle is made of several hard objects, such as seed pods, deer hooves, or shells, strung together on a hoop, a rope, or a wooden frame.

The third type is the notched-stick rattle, also called rasping stick or morache. This is not a rattle at all in the usual sense of the word. It consists of a stick with notches running the length of one side. Against this notched stick a second, smooth stick is rubbed back and forth, giving a scraping, buzzing, or rumbling sound. Notched-stick rattles are used in the American Southwest—and also in China.

This, incidentally, is only one of several features that seem to link the music of western North America with that of China and Japan. Others are the use of stone gongs and the tendency to shift the pitch upward in the middle

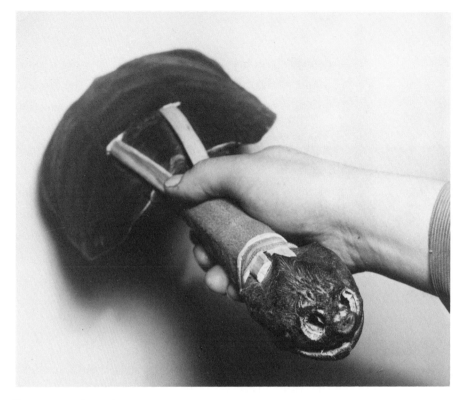

Iroquois turtle rattle made in 1976.

27

of a song. Here again, as in the case of supposed European and African influences on the music of the Eastern Woodlands, we cannot be sure that an actual connection exists.

On the other hand, if the world's music were lumped into super-large geographical areas, the Americas would probably be included with eastern Asia, not so much because of the features just mentioned but because of similarities in vocal tension (the tight throat) and in the use of limited diatonic scales (see page 15).

Flutes and Whistles

Most Indian flutes are not flutes at all, but flageolets. The flageolet, also called whistle flute, flûte à bec, or block flute, has a whistle mouthpiece like the so-called recorder that was used in Europe in the Middle Ages and has recently become popular again in the United States. Typical flageolet melodies are given on pages 79 and 81.

If the flageolet has no finger holes it is called a whistle.

Flute Song at sunrise, Hopi.

Sometimes carved out of bird bones, whistles are typically used to make contact with the spirit world, especially in religious ceremonies.

True flutes have no whistle mouthpiece at all. But instead of being blown across a hole near one end, as in the

Flute-Song Prelude

HOPI

Sung by Masaveimah and Kavanhongevah,
about 1905

modern concert flute, Indian flutes are blown across the very end itself—just as you can produce a flutelike tone by blowing across the top of a bottle. A Hopi melody played by large end-blown flutes is given on this page. This piece of music is supposed to bring rain and is unusual in that it is played by several flutes in unison with human voices.

When two or more flutes are tied together, the instrument is called a syrinx or a panpipes. These are rare north of Mexico. The mysterious Haida instrument shown on page 30 is possibly a syrinx, though the individual pipes in this case may be flageolets or may even at one time have contained vibrating reeds, as in the modern clarinet.

Cree moose hunter with
birchbark horn.

Old Haida wind instrument dug
up on a farm in the Queen
Charlotte Islands.

Horns

Horns are made of clay, wood, birchbark, or large
conch shells. These are quite uncommon. Mostly they are
used by hunters to call game or by warriors to terrorize
the enemy.

Stringed Instruments

The musical bow, formerly used in the Far West, was
played like a Jew's harp. It looked something like an

ordinary hunting bow. You would hold it against your mouth and pluck the string. By varying the opening of your mouth you could vary the pitch. It is said that this very quiet instrument was used by lovers.

The Human Voice as an Instrument

In many parts of North America the voice itself is used to accompany singing. In certain Yuman songs people grunt rhythmically while others sing. In northwestern California there are songs in which a male chorus chants a rhythm in the bass while a woman singer carries the melody. Many tribes have songs in which the men carry the melody while the women sing a continuous high note called the "drone."

All tribes have songs in which the melody is carried not by ordinary words but by euphonic, or musical, syllables. This in fact is typical of Indian singing generally and is found in most of the songs in this book. Such syllables are not entirely meaningless. When we sing *fa la la la la* in the carol "Deck the Halls," the syllables actually suggest gaiety or festivity. It would be unthinkable to include them in a serious or prayerful song.

In the same way, syllables used in Indian songs often have a certain vague meaning. Notice the syllables in the Cherokee lullaby, page 34, and in the Sioux war song, page 73. Could you imagine using the lullaby syllables *ma ma ma* in the war song? Probably not.

Songs for the Very Young

Among the Crow Indians of Montana it is believed that women used to learn lullabies from animals. If a woman happened to be passing by a wolf's den while the mother wolf was singing to her cubs she would stop and listen. When she returned home she would sing the song to her own children. Among the Cherokee of Tennessee and North Carolina, hunters were said to have learned lullabies from female bears in exactly the same manner.

Songs for children can be obtained from other kinds of animals as well. The people of Isleta Pueblo in New Mexico have a lullaby that is supposed to be sung by the horned toad when she puts her children to sleep. This song has no words, they say, "because the horned toad cannot talk."

Beetles Go Riding

By no means do all Indian lullabies come from animals or talk about animals. Yet songs of this type are very common.

A Pueblo mother sometimes sings to her baby as though she and the baby were beetles. "Go to sleep, my little beetle," sings the Zuni mother. And the Hopi mother sings, "Beetles go riding on each other's backs down along the trail." By this the mother means that she carries her baby on her back just as beetles sometimes ride on each other's backs as they crawl along. This lullaby is given on page 33. The words are childlike, but the music is sophisticated, displaying the complexity of Hopi music at its best.

Sleep Song

HOPI

Sung by Clarence Taptuka,
about 1950

ho - ho - yao - woŏ_____ nao - ikw - yo - kyang - o_____
Bee - tles go_____ rid - ing on each o - ther's backs_____

zhoŏ - pe pa - ve_____ pu - va_____ pu - va_____
down a - long__ the trail_____ sleep_____ sleep_____

pu - va_____ pu - va ve ve ve ve ve ve ve ve ve ve ve ve
sleep_____ sleep_____ a - long a - long a - long a - long a - long a -

ve ve ve ve ve_____ ve ve ve ve ve ve ve ve ve ve.
long - a a - long__ a - long a - long a - long a - long a - long - a

*repeat twice with variations
indicated on p. 106*

hohoyaowoŏ: beetles | *naoikwyokyango*: they carry each other on their backs | *zhoŏpe pave*: on the trail | *puva*: sleep | *ve ve etc.*:
meaningless

33

Lullaby

CHEROKEE

Moderato ($\quad$ = 84)

Sung by Tom Handle, about 1950

1. ŏŏ - stĭ - e   ta-ka-hla - ne   ma ma ma   ka__ ka   ne   ŏŏ - stĭ - e   he-ka-hla-hska
   Lit - tle one,   go   to sleep,   ma ma ma,   ka__ ka nay,   lit - tle one,   sleep - y one.

2. ma ma ma   a   ve   a   ŏŏ - stĭ - e   ta-ka-hla - ne   ma ma ma   ka   ka   ne.
   Ma ma ma,   ah vay ah,   lit - tle one,   go   to sleep,   ma ma ma,   ka   ka nay.

ŏŏ-stĭ-e: little one, baby | *ta-ka-hla-ni*: he is going to sleep | *ma ma ma, ka ka ne*: meaningless | *he-ah*: this one | *ga-ka-hla-hska*: he is sleepy | *a ve a*: meaningless? (Notice that some of the words are pronounced differently when sung.)

Simple Lullabies

In many Indian lullabies both the words and the music are very simple. This kind of lullaby is found in tribes all over North America and may belong to an extremely old kind of music that survives mainly in storytelling songs and lullabies. The Cherokee lullaby on this page a good example.

Notice that this song, like most of the other lullabies in this book, was recorded not by a woman but by a man. Although Cherokee men do compose lullabies, it is pos-sible that the man learned this song from his mother or some other woman. The point is that when non-Indians go into an Indian village asking for songs, they don't always get a chance to hear women singers. In many Indian communities it would be considered improper for a woman to sing for strangers.

In Navajo country this is true to such an extent that one well-known student of Navajo music flatly stated that there are no Navajo lullabies. This person was a man. The anthropologist Gladys Reichard, however, was able to report that the Navajo do indeed have lullabies.

Cradle Songs

In most Indian tribes babies are strapped to a cradleboard for easy handling. The cradleboard can be carried on an older person's back, laid on the ground, or hung by a rope from a tree.

Babies in hanging cradleboards are soothed to sleep by cradle songs. The mother, an older sister, or some other person attaches a string to the cradle and sits at a little distance holding the free end. As the sitter pulls the string forth, then lets it back, pulls it forth, then lets it back, she croons a cradle song. The baby, she hopes, will soon fall asleep.

In the old days the Kwakiutl Indians of British Columbia lived in large wooden houses alongside the sea. Out front would be totem poles boasting of the honors the family had won or inherited. Inside would be pillars supporting massive roof beams and, in the middle of the floor, a fire directly beneath an opening in the roof. From one of the roof beams the Kwakiutl mother would swing her baby, singing the cradle song given on page 36. Notice

Crow mother with baby
on cradleboard.

Cradle Song

KWAKIUTL

Slow and crooning (♩ = 69)   Anonymous, about 1905

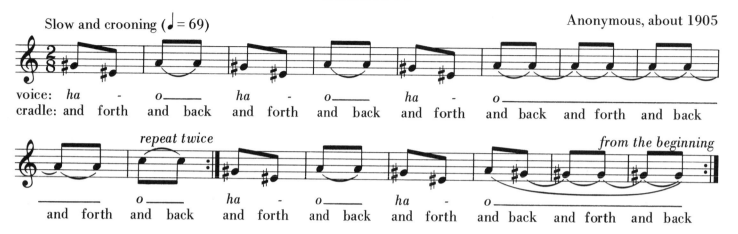

voice: ha - o_____ ha - o_____ ha - o _____

cradle: and forth   and back   and forth   and back   and forth   and back   and forth   and back

repeat twice   *from the beginning*

_____   o _____   ha - o _____   ha - o _____

and forth   and back   and forth   and back   and forth   and back   and forth   and back

that the cradle is pulled on the offbeat, just as the drum is struck on the offbeat in many Northwest Coast songs. Compare the examples on pages 86 and 89.

Laughing Songs

Along the Northwest Coast, people used to believe that a baby had to be kept happy. Otherwise it would get discouraged and die.

It was with this fear in mind, perhaps, that mothers and fathers sang special songs to their infant children, en-couraging them to grow up and become adults. A father would sing to his little boy, telling him of the duties and privileges he would have someday as a hunter or fisherman. And the mother would sing to her little girl, imagining the day when the child would already be grown, saying, "She will pick berries" or "She will gather wild roses."

Often these songs have touches of humor intended to make the child laugh. The parent might sing to the child, "I am your slave" or "I am your dog." In the Tsimshian song given on page 38 the music itself suggests laughter.

Tsimshian village with
totem poles.

Lullaby for a Girl

TSIMSHIAN

Sung by Pelha, called Robert Pearl,
about 1927

temram: will only gather | sakalamps: (wild) roses | tralkyalkum: the little child | hanak: woman | kanwĭltkudiwitkot: that's why she was born

Notice that the laughing refrain gives way to a different kind of music when the verse begins. The verse is pure recitative—musical talking—as in many Eskimo songs. When the singer Robert Pearl recorded this song he sang it seven times, changing the verse with each repetition. For the words "gather wild roses" the following phrases were substituted, with the seventh verse merely a repetition of the first.

2 | dig wild rice
3 | get hemlock sap
4 | pick strawberries
5 | pick soapberries
6 | pick elderberries
7 | gather wild roses

In addition, the rhythm and melody of the verse, but not of the refrain, were changed somewhat with each repetition, making for a rather long, complicated song in true Northwest Coast style.

Storytelling

At the start of winter, when the days have grown short, the people of Picuris Pueblo say that the earth goes to sleep for a period of about a month. This is the time for telling stories. Inside the adobe houses, children gather around a parent or grandparent to hear tales of Fish Maiden, Old Coyote, Big Nostril, Morning Star, or the cannibal giant.

Like many other Indian myths and tales, Picuris children's stories include songs. These songs occur at important points in the narrative and are always sung by one of the characters, whose part is played by the storyteller. This is the typical Indian way of mixing songs with stories. Only in rare cases will an entire story, including both narrative and dialogue, be sung or chanted. Chanted stories have been collected among the Ute, the Pawnee, and the Penobscot. But although they are probably more common than is generally believed, no examples have so far been found in the pueblos.

In the Picuris story of the giant and the elf, the elf's song is particularly interesting because it acts as a magical device to help the elf defeat the giant. The story is here given in its entirety.

The Giant and the Elf

Long, long ago there used to be a giant who came to people's houses and stole the children. He put them in his pack basket and carried them off to his home.

Now, in those days the elf was living on Jicarita Mountain, and one day the giant came up the mountain looking for children and saw the elf.

"Come, get into my basket," he said.

"Why?" said the elf.

"I said get into my basket! If you don't do it, I'll catch you and put you there." Then he picked up the elf, put him into the basket, and started off for home. Inside the basket the elf began to sing. As he sang, the basket went up and down, up and down, and this is the song he sang.

(Sing "The Elf's Song"
with repeat and first verse only.)

The giant couldn't hear the singing inside the basket, but he could feel the basket bouncing up and down. It made the basket seem very heavy, and by the time he got home he was dripping with sweat and all tired out. Right away he lay down and took a nap.

While he was sleeping, the elf climbed out of the basket and discovered a big pile of bones. As it happened, he had his medicine bag with him. So he took out a little medicine, chewed it, and spit it on the bones. Then he

Some of the oldest buildings
in Picuris Pueblo.

said to the bones, "Little children, get up!" And immediately all the children the giant had eaten came back to life and stood up.

Right away he sent two of the children to find him some pitch. They returned very soon with what he wanted. Then all the children who had been brought back to life rubbed the magic pitch on the elf's body so that the giant

41

The Elf's Song

PICURIS

Allegro (♩ = 116)

Sung by Rosendo Vargas, about 1920

we - se - lo____ we - se - lo se - lo se lo____ se

lo we - 'a me - 'e ye - he ye - he -

he 'a - 'a - ha - a - a 'e - he - lo - we

1. 'o - wi - t'a-i - nă - lŭ-'e-pa ta-so-'el - hu-cha-men - no sa
   Some-one ve - ry kind_ is car-ry-ing__ me on his back____ O.____
2. 'o - wi - t'a-i - nă - lŭ-'e-pa nă wi-lun - na____ ta-so-ta-ki-an-no____
   Some-one ve - ry kind_ has put me in a nice__ warm_ place____ O.____

weselo etc.: meaningless | *'owit'a-inălŭ-'epa*: a person who is very kind | *taso'elhu chamenno sa*: is carrying me on his back | *nă wilunna tasotakianno*: has put me in a warm place | *As a variation these four beats may be omitted

would not be able to kill him. When this had been done, the elf turned the children back into bones.

Now the giant woke up and stirred the fire with his poker stick. "Oh, there you are, my little one," he said to the elf. Then he said to himself, "Tonight I'll have a nice dinner. This little boy looks fat." Then he put the elf in the fire to roast.

As the elf went into the fire, he chewed a little of the medicine from his medicine bag and spit it on the flames. Then he began to sing. "Why, this little boy sings very well," said the giant, and he lay back and listened to the song.

(Sing "The Elf's Song"
with repeat and second verse only.)

By the time the elf had finished singing, the giant was sound asleep. Then the elf, with sparks flying, came out of the fire. He picked up the poker stick and hit the giant on the head and killed him.

Once again he spit medicine on the bones, and all the children began to rise up. He said to the children, "I've killed the old giant who's been eating you up. Now you can go home to your parents, who are thinking about you. I too have a home far away and a grandmother there who is thinking about me. I must go. You go too." They all started out.

And from that time on there were no more giants.

Prayers and Magic

"I may pray with my mouth and the prayer will be heard, but if I sing the prayer it will be heard sooner by Wakantanka." These words, spoken many years ago by the Sioux prayer maker Red Weasel, call attention to two ideas about Indian music that are as important today among traditional Indian groups as they were in Red Weasel's time.

The first is that song does not come from the mouth but from somewhere within the singer's body. As pointed out in an earlier chapter, when you sing Indian songs you should keep the sound in your throat. Try it with the Delaware "Peyote Song" given on page 97. When you have learned the song, sing it in front of a mirror with your mouth slightly open but without moving either your lips or your teeth. You will have the strange sensation of hearing music without being able to see where it comes from. The song issues from your body as if by magic. (Such an experiment exaggerates what is in fact only a tendency. Indian singers usually display lip movement, but they keep it to a minimum.)

The second idea is that singing has the power to make things happen. This too has been pointed out in an earlier chapter. It accounts for the fact that almost all Indian rituals and ceremonies include some form of singing. Coming from deep within the singer's body, the sound issuing forth seems to exert an influence on the forces of nature, thus helping to make the singer's wish, or prayer, come true.

For Personal Success

The traditional Indian method of acquiring power is to seek a vision or dream in which a spirit, usually an animal, speaks a brief message in the form of a song. If a bear spirit appears, it generally brings success in curing disease. An eagle spirit brings success in war or hunting. Later, at any time in his life, the dreamer may increase his personal power by singing the song that was given to him by his animal helper.

But vision power seldom comes without effort. A com- mon way of seeking it is to abstain from food for several days, thereby demonstrating to the spirits that you are willing to make a sacrifice.

In the old days the most dramatic vision quests were those of the Plains Indians. If a man wished for power, he would fast in the wilderness for a period of four days, all the while crying for help to the Great Mystery, called Wakantanka by the Sioux or Wakonda by the Omaha. Sometimes he might remove thin strips of flesh from his body or even cut off a finger as a sign of his devotion.

Among the Omaha a boy's first vision quest was an

Crying to Wakonda

OMAHA

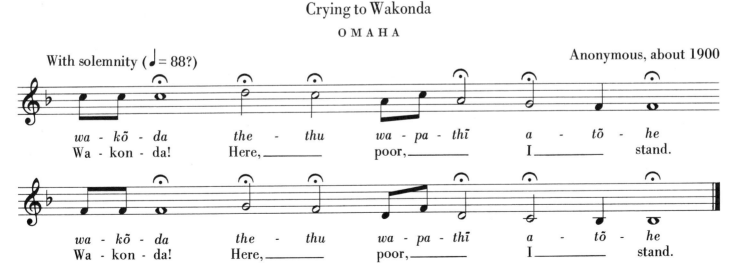

With solemnity ($\bullet$ = 88?)

Anonymous, about 1900

wa - kõ - da   the - thu   wa - pa - thĩ   a - tõ - he
Wa - kon - da!   Here,_____   poor,_____   I_____   stand.

wa - kõ - da   the - thu   wa - pa - thĩ   a - tõ - he
Wa - kon - da!   Here,_____   poor,_____   I_____   stand.

wakõnda: Wakonda (the supreme spirit) | *thethu*: here | *wapathĩ*: poor, needy | *atõhe*: he stands, and I am he

especially important occasion. His parents would prepare him for it by teaching him the song given on page 45. They would then smear his head with clay and send him out into the wilds without food. For four days he would cry his song to Wakonda, tears running down his face. He would wipe the tears with his palms and lift his wet hands to the sky, then lay them down on the earth. Finally he would fall unconscious, and in his sleep Wakonda would send an animal to bring him a new song. The power song of the eagle, given on page 47, though it does not come from the Omaha, is the kind of song that would be received in such a vision.

For Good Hunting

Power songs received in visions can be helpful not only to the individual but to his family, his friends, or even the whole tribe. In the Eastern Woodlands, parents used to send their little children, both boys and girls, out into the forest so that they might bring back a vision that would increase the family's power. If, for example, a boy re-ceived hunting power, it would benefit everybody.

The Nez Percé of Idaho also observed the custom of sending children into the wilderness. Children, being "pure," were uniquely qualified to receive vision power. Adults were "impure" in that they had experienced sexual relations and were therefore not likely to be favored by the spirits.

A Nez Percé girl might see a pelican in her vision. From such a spirit she would receive healing power. A boy might see an eagle and receive a song like the one given on page 47, which would make him a good hunter. The man who had received this particular song as a boy added the following comments, which describe the picture that the song created in his mind.

"The sun is low, so that it strikes just the upper part of one side of the canyon wall. In the bottom of the canyon Deer are browsing. When the little Deer sees Eagle soaring above, he starts to run, and the Eagle begins to sing. When the fawn gets a little distance ahead, Eagle sings the word *toward-you-my-song*, and the fawn stops to listen to the song. Eagle soars over him, circling about. The Deer looks up and is unable to move. Eagle swoops

Power Song of the Eagle

NEZ PERCE

Deliberately (♪ = 138)

Sung by Ralph Armstrong, 1909

hai - yi - la_____ hi - yi hi - yi hi - yi hai - yi - la ao - nă - tu - iq -
Tilt - ing down,_____ wing - ing, wing - ing, wing - ing, tilt - ing down_ toward you my

nă - nis hi - yi hi - yi hi - yi hai - yi la a - wi - yi - hi - yi hai - yi - la
song is wing - ing, wing - ing, wing - ing, tilt - ing down,_____ soar - ing, wing - ing, tilt - ing down.

haiyila: tilting on wings | *hiyi*: flapping | *aonătuiqnănis*: pursuing by means of song | *awiyihiyi*: soaring

down on the fawn, and the smaller birds of prey flock to the feast."

Eagle power was much desired by Indians of all tribes, and all kinds of sacred ornaments were made of eagle feathers, bones, and claws. In the West, eagles used to be caught live by placing fresh meat as bait on a loose grill-work of sticks laid over a pit. The eagle catcher, hiding in the pit, reached up and grasped the eagle's leg as it settled down to feed on the meat. An eagle captured in this manner is shown on page 48.

For Healing

Disease may be cured by calling upon spirits known to have medicine power. In most cases the call, or prayer,

Placating the spirit of a slain
eagle, Assiniboin.

takes the form of a song. Sometimes, as among the Sioux,
the singer asks his spirit helper to send a "voice," which
may mean that the singer wishes to feel—or hear—the
spirit's presence.

In Iroquois country special curing ceremonies, with
music and dance, are held every year at midwinter. At
this time men who belong to the society of Faces put on
their masks and proceed to the meeting house. As they
enter the house, their leader, singing the "Dream Song"
given on page 49, announces his belief that a "voice" is
already present. In some versions of the song the words
are "a voice is floating." The version given here, however, has "a voice is rising." Probably this refers to the
voice of the Great Face that lives in the West and has the
power to heal. The maskers entering the house represent
this spirit and his helpers—who are not animals but
weird humans with twisted or grinning faces.

When the Faces are all inside, other songs are sung,
there is dancing, and people who wish to be cured have
the Faces blow ashes into their hair, thus allowing themselves to be symbolically purified by the fire from which
the ashes have been taken. Later the Faces may visit the

Dream Song

IROQUOIS

Sung by Joshua "Billy" Buck, 1941

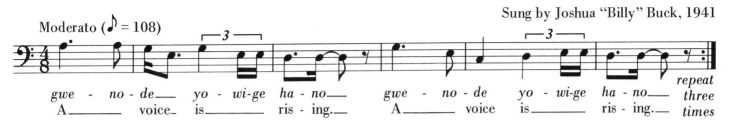

Moderato (♪ = 108)

gwe - no - de____ yo - wi-ge ha - no____ gwe - no - de____ yo - wi-ge ha - no____ *repeat*
A____ voice_ is____ ris - ing.____ A____ voice_ is____ ris - ing.____ *three*
times

guwennode: a voice | *yowige*: is rising | *hano*: meaningless

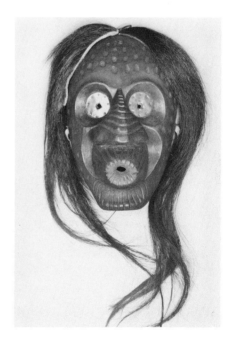

Iroquois Faces. *Left* | with typical twisted features. *Right* | with pock marks and blowing mouth.

49

Their leader sings "Dream Song"
as the Faces enter an Iroquois
home at midwinter.

homes of individual families. Each time they enter a house their leader sings "Dream Song."

To Control the Weather

When the Yuma Indians of Arizona used to go to war, their medicine men would go with them singing "lightning songs" to bring down a storm on the enemy. When Sioux warriors approached an enemy camp, their medicine man would sing in order to bring a drizzling rain to cover their attack. In most cases, however, weather magic was used to bring not bad weather but good weather, which meant sunshine in the North and rain in the dry Southwest. Many if not most Pueblo songs, even today, are prayers for rain.

On both the Atlantic and Pacific coasts people had special songs to quiet rough waters. Among the Eskimos,

Anivyunna singing with
a hand drum.

To Quiet a Raging Storm
COPPER ESKIMO

tao kisuma qailutin uviaiyuyain: man outside there pray come, pray make your entrance (into me)

51

Singing moccasin-game songs with
a hand drum, Chippewa.

To Win the Game

Games are played with great seriousness, and special songs, chants, or even instrumental music may be performed to bring success. As in modern college and high school football, women are sometimes asked to do the chanting while men play the game. Often the players themselves perform the chants, which either bring good luck to the chanter or bad luck to his opponents.

One of the most popular Indian pastimes is the moccasin game. In this game two teams of several men each sit facing each other about five or six feet apart. The team whose turn it is to play hides a pebble or some other small object in one of four moccasins laid out in a row between the teams. While the opposing team tries to guess where the pebble is, the team that has hidden it sings a song to unnerve the guessers. The game is not always as simple as it looks. There are elaborate rules and a complicated scoring system.

Among the Navajo the moccasin game reenacts a myth. In the ancient days, so the story goes, the game was played

songs to quiet a storm or to make the sun come out were extremely common. A weather song sung by the young Copper Eskimo, Anivyunna, is given on page 51.

The words to Anivyunna's song are not addressed to the storm itself, as might seem, but to Anivyunna's guardian spirit. The spirit enters the singer's body, it is hoped, thus giving him power to subdue the storm.

Dove Song

NAVAJO

Anonymous, about 1887

Andante (♩ = 66?)

wosh— wosh— nai - thi - la 'a 'a wosh— wosh— nai - thi - lo 'o 'o
Coo— Coo— picks them up up up. Coo— Coo— picks them up up up.

wosh— wosh— nai - thi - la 'a 'a tsi - nol - ka - zhi nai - thi - la 'a 'a
Coo— Coo— picks them up up up. Glos - sy Locks— picks them up up up.

ke - hli - chi - chi nai - thi - la 'a 'a wosh— wosh— nai - thi - lo 'o 'o
Red Moc - ca - sin picks them up up up. Coo— Coo— picks them up up up.

wosh wosh: coo coo (name for the dove) | *naithila*: picks them up (seeds) | *tsinolkazhi*: glossy locks | *kehlichichi*: red moccasins

to settle an argument between the day animals, who wanted the sun to shine all the time, and the nocturnal animals, who wanted perpetual night. Because the game ended in a tie, day and night have been of equal length ever since.

While the animals were playing, naturally they sang moccasin-game songs. Each of these songs made fun of an animal of the opposing team. The song mocking the dove went like this:

Coo Coo picks them up,
Coo Coo picks them up,
Glossy Locks picks them up,
Red Moccasin picks them up.

The dove is here called Coo Coo just as a dog might be called Bow Wow, though to Navajo ears the dove's call is *wosh wosh*. Doves hop along the ground picking up seeds. They have glossy plumage and red feet. If you were a dove you might find this song somewhat irritating, especially if it were sung in a taunting manner.

When Navajo players sing the "Dove Song," it is as though they are mocking the man from the opposing team who is at the moment trying to guess where the pebble is hidden. This song, given on page 53, is only one of many hundreds of animal songs used in the Navajo moccasin game.

Dances

Just as songs may be prayers set to music, dances may often be thought of as prayers put into action. The importance of Indian rain dances and war dances, for example, is well known: these performances are really prayers for rain or for success on the warpath. But there are many other kinds of dances as well, dances to drive out disease, to make corn grow, to bring success in hunting, to renew the world at the end of winter, or to give thanks to a spirit helper.

Most Indian dances are group dances, commonly performed in a circle, with the dancers either facing the center of the circle or facing forward in a circular file. In the Eastern Woodlands and in the Southwest these circular dances, or round dances, almost always proceed in a counterclockwise direction. See the diagram on page 61. In the Plains area and in northern California the

dancers usually move clockwise.

Dances in which the participants form straight lines are almost nonexistent in the East but fairly common in the Southwest and on the Plains. Solo dances are hardly found at all in the East but occur on the Plains and, especially, on the Northwest Coast and in the Eskimo area, where solo dancing is more common than group dancing.

Rarely do men and women dance together in sacred or ceremonial dances. It would not be proper to do so, at least not in traditional Indian communities. If both sexes join in a single dance, they are usually segregated as in the Iroquois Drum Dance shown on page 61. The men's and women's steps described for this dance are typical in that the women shuffle along with very little leg movement, while the men lift their knees and stomp their heels in a performance that is felt to be definitely masculine.

Animal Dances

Nearly all tribes have dances that pay tribute to animals. In the East such dances are astonishingly numerous. Fish dances, bear dances, raccoon dances, lizard dances, snake dances, robin dances, and many others are regularly performed. In recent years the Iroquois have even kept up their Pigeon Dance, in honor of the extinct passenger pigeon.

In many of these dances the animal itself is imitated by ingenious arm and body movements that really do suggest a bear, a snake, a robin, or whatever animal is being honored. On the Plains and in the Southwest the effect is heightened by the wearing of animal costumes, especially in bear, buffalo, and deer dances.

The Diegueño of southern California, like most other tribes in the extreme Southwest, have dances performed to animal song-cycles, which typically refer to the story of an animal's journey across the land. A song from the Wildcat Dance is given on the opposite page.

The Wildcat Dance is performed by men only, facing each other in two straight lines. It did not originate with the Diegueño but was learned by them from either the Yuma or the Mojave. The words to the songs, unintelligible to us, are equally unintelligible to the Diegueño, who don't mind in the least—just as English-speaking audiences endure or even insist upon opera sung in Italian. The words probably refer to the wildcat but are untranslatable and must be regarded as meaningless syllables.

Among the Mojave, wildcats are supposed to have power over game animals. Possibly the Wildcat Dance was originally a prayer for good hunting.

Dances of Appreciation

Although animal dances may be performed to make a specific wish come true, in many cases they simply express thanks or appreciation for the benefits people have enjoyed. Nor are animals the only recipients of such dances. Among the Choctaw a dance used to be performed in honor of trees, thanking them for their cool shade.

A Song of the Wildcat Dance

DIEGUEÑO

Sung by Mrs. Kate Coleman, 1927

eme shaiyo-e etc.: Yuman words, not understood by the Diegueño. Meaning unknown.

Choctaw Snake Dance.

Water drum and horn rattle used in Iroquois Drum Dance.

Among the Iroquois certain dances are addressed directly to the supreme spirit in the sky. It is said that these dances "belong" to the Creator. They express both thanks and joy with regard to all the blessings of life and are believed to have been invented in the heavens.

One of these dances is the Drum Dance, also called Thanksgiving Dance or Worship Dance, performed to a series of as many as fifty songs. An unusually beautiful Drum Dance song is given on page 59, with dance steps explained on pages 60–61. Although this is a sacred dance, it is not considered improper for non-Indians to perform it. In fact, if outsiders are present, they may be asked to join in.

A Song of the Drum Dance

IROQUOIS

Leader: Corbett Sundown, 1959

The Drum Dance in Performance

See music on page 59

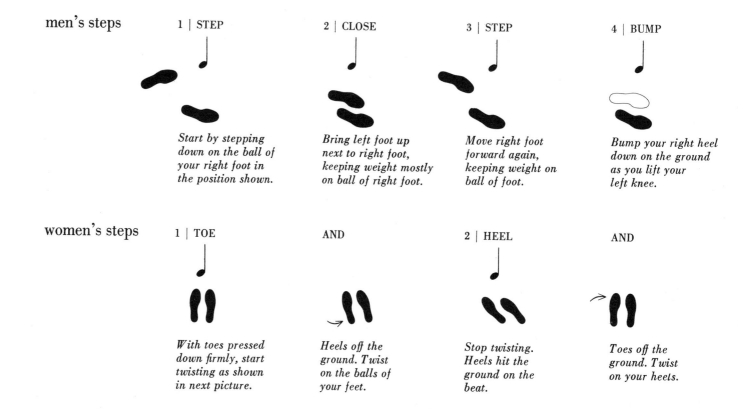

men's steps

1 | STEP
Start by stepping down on the ball of your right foot in the position shown.

2 | CLOSE
Bring left foot up next to right foot, keeping weight mostly on ball of right foot.

3 | STEP
Move right foot forward again, keeping weight on ball of foot.

4 | BUMP
Bump your right heel down on the ground as you lift your left knee.

women's steps

1 | TOE
With toes pressed down firmly, start twisting as shown in next picture.

AND
Heels off the ground. Twist on the balls of your feet.

2 | HEEL
Stop twisting. Heels hit the ground on the beat.

AND
Toes off the ground. Twist on your heels.

arm and body movements | men and women

Men improvise arm movements, wave arms like wings, act as though charging, etc.

Women keep knees slightly bent throughout. Each time toe or heel comes down, knees react by bending just a little more, so that the dancer's body has a slight pumping motion as she moves along.

Women keep all movements small. Elbows at sides. Swing forearms left and right, then up and down. Then raise elbows level with shoulders and rotate wrists. These gestures imitate the work women do in the garden.

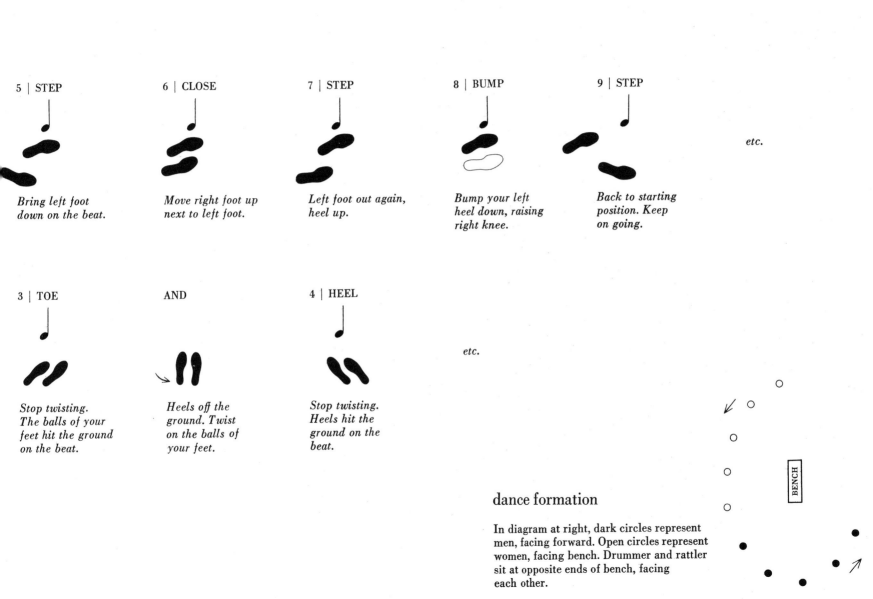

5 | STEP

Bring left foot down on the beat.

6 | CLOSE

Move right foot up next to left foot.

7 | STEP

Left foot out again, heel up.

8 | BUMP

Bump your left heel down, raising right knee.

9 | STEP

Back to starting position. Keep on going.

etc.

3 | TOE

Stop twisting. The balls of your feet hit the ground on the beat.

AND

Heels off the ground. Twist on the balls of your feet.

4 | HEEL

Stop twisting. Heels hit the ground on the beat.

etc.

dance formation

In diagram at right, dark circles represent men, facing forward. Open circles represent women, facing bench. Drummer and rattler sit at opposite ends of bench, facing each other.

BENCH

Komugi, a Kwakiutl dancing mask.

People who have old-style costumes—beadwork, buckskin shirts, or feather headdresses—wear them during the Drum Dance, but it is not necessary to do so. Nor is it necessary to perform the steps accurately. If you don't know how to do them, you may simply walk along. Such an attitude points to the remarkable sense of democracy for which the eastern Indians have been famous since colonial times. It is in marked contrast to the native attitude toward dancing in the Southwest, where everything has to be perfect.

Masked Dances

Masked dances are performed to some extent in all regions but are most highly developed in the Southwest and along the Northwest Coast. Northwest Coast masks, carved of wood and elaborately painted, are easily the most intricate, and perhaps the most beautiful, in North America. A typical example is shown on this page.

Masked dances are mysterious and deliberately frightening. Although the mask may sometimes represent an animal spirit, it usually portrays a divine human being —a god or goddess—often monstrous in appearance. As the dance progresses, it is as though the god has come to earth and is exhibiting his power.

Among the Navajo the most famous masked dances are those of the Night Chant, a nine-day healing ceremony that ends in an all-night celebration with continuous singing and frequent dancing. It is as though the gods and goddesses themselves, who have been repeatedly summoned during the first eight days of the ceremony, have at last made their appearance. By their dancing they help cure the sick person for whom the ceremony is being conducted.

This final dance of the Night Chant, often called the Yeibitchai Dance, is performed by an equal number of gods and goddesses, who form a pair of straight lines as shown in the native sand painting reproduced on this page. The leader of the dance is the Yeibitchai himself, pronounced YAY-bitch-eye ("Grandfather-of-the-Gods"). He is shown as the first dancer on the left in the top row. The

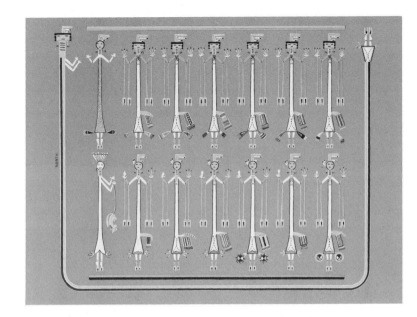

Night Chant dancers as depicted in a Navajo sand painting.

fourteen dancers are enclosed on three sides by the elongated body of a rainbow with legs, arms, and a face. The rainbow, which "protects" the dancers from evil influences, is represented only in the sand painting, not in the actual dance.

Yeibitchai songs are well known even outside of Navajo country. With their driving rhythms and eerie melodies from the spirit world they are perhaps the only type of Navajo music that readily appeals to outsiders.

At this moment a Yeibitchai song very much like the one given on this page is speeding through space toward a faraway galaxy where, perhaps forty thousand years from now, it may be presented to intelligent star-creatures as

A Dance Song of the Night Chant

NAVAJO

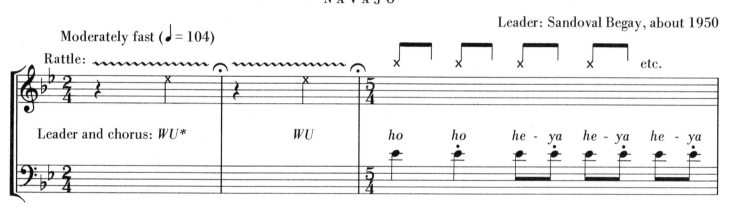

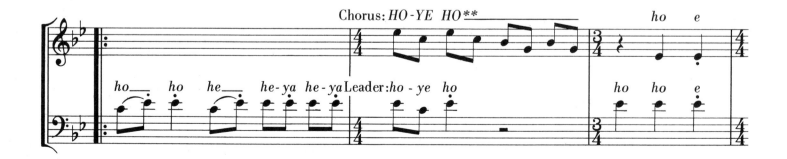

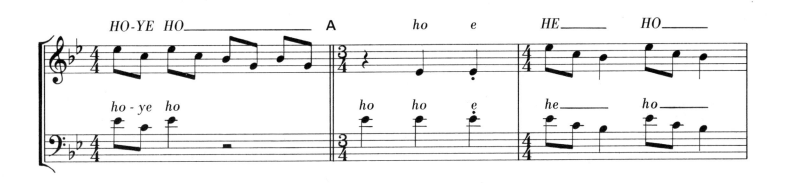

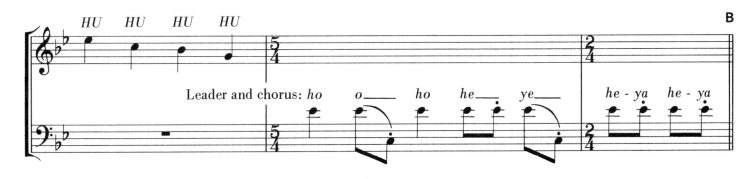

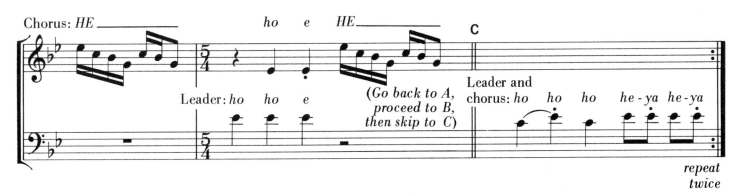

WU: a falsetto howl, somewhat reminiscent of a dog's or coyote's howl | **Syllables printed in capitals are sung in an eerie falsetto

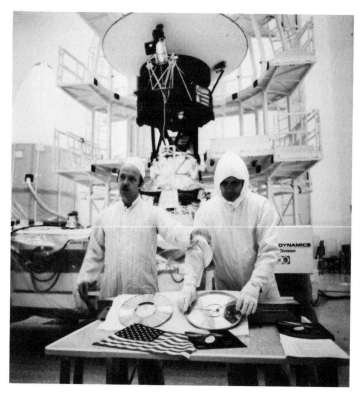

A song of the Night Chant is included in this "Sounds of the Earth" recording about to be placed aboard the Voyager spacecraft.

a "sound" of the planet Earth. The "Sounds of the Earth" recording, which includes selections from Bach and Beethoven, as well as the Night Chant, was sent up with the Voyager spacecraft in the summer of 1977 in the hope of making contact with another world.

Pleasure Dances

Not all dances are sacred. Some are strictly for pleasure, and in these dances men and women may face each other, hold hands, or intermingle. None of which would be permissible in sacred dances.

The song given on page 67 is a pleasure dance song commonly heard among the Penobscot Indians during the early years of the century. By the 1950s the Penobscot had all but forgotten their native dances. Then, in the 1970s, the dances were revived as part of a general Penobscot awakening that has included a well-publicized claim to vast tracts of land in the old tribal territory now in the state of Maine.

Another pleasure dance song, from the Choctaw, is

Dance Song

PENOBSCOT

Anonymous, about 1910

Pleasure Dance

C H O C T A W

Sung by Sidney Wesley, 1933

repeat
ad lib.

given on page 68. In this dance the men and women face each other in two rows, moving their arms up and down as though shaking corn in a basket. The rhythm is provided by a most unusual Indian instrument: the striking stick. The player holds one stick in each hand and beats out the rhythm by striking one against the other.

If you play this piece on the piano, fitting all three parts together, you will get a delightful rhythmic effect reminiscent of African music. But this will be not quite correct, because the striking-stick rhythm should not be coordinated with the melody. It should be perfectly independent, so that it may be free to get a little ahead of, or lag slightly behind, the melody. The striking sticks provide a ground texture, not a true counterpoint. This can be most easily achieved by having one group sing the melody, another group give the response ("Ha!"), and a third group beat out the rhythm.

War Songs

In former times war was a permanent fact of life for nearly every Indian tribe in North America. Villages were constantly in danger of attack, and when the moment came even women and children joined in the defense as barricades were hastily thrown up.

On another day the same village would be sending its warriors out to avenge the wrongs they had suffered— or merely to seize food, horses, or other property if their own supplies were running short. The mounting of a war party called for songs to insure success, songs of farewell as the warriors departed, and, upon their return, songs to celebrate their bravery.

Starting on the Warpath

If a young man simply wished to demonstrate his courage, he might slip away with a few companions and make a raid on some distant village for the purpose of snatching a horse or quickly killing an unwary victim, whose scalp would be brought home as a trophy.

But if a larger war party were called for, and if they expected to be met by the enemy in open combat, elaborate ceremonies might be held, with singing and even dancing. Among the Plains Indians, departing warriors would put on that peculiar finery, especially the feathered war bonnet, which has come to be thought of as typical Indian dress by people the world over. In addition a

Sioux warrior might have his face painted with war paint, often by a medicine man.

In about 1912 the Teton Sioux warrior Bear Eagle recalled the song given on page 73. It had been sung for him years earlier by the medicine man Little Buffalo, while painting Bear Eagle's forehead with a blue stripe that ended in branches on each cheekbone. As in many Indian songs, the singer in this case speaks as though he were someone else. As he sings, it is as though the warrior himself were singing. "Clear the way! In a sacred manner I come!" (Among the Plains Indians war was regarded as an act of devotion to the supreme spirit.)

You will notice that the first syllable of the English word "sacred" is difficult to sing as a sixteenth note. It is much easier to get the proper effect if you use the Sioux words. You must realize that starting a beat like this with a very short note is a means of accentuation. It is not a true syncopation.

Farewell to the Warriors

The actual moment of departure is charged with emotion. The warrior setting out may never again see his parents or the woman he loves. During the long days on the warpath he will think of home.

Among the Kiowa it is said that lonely warriors used to sing "wind songs," which expressed their loneliness while out on the plains where nothing could be heard but the wind.

Many of the most typical love songs sung by Indian women are addressed to warriors about to depart. Just as in Chinese love poetry, the favorite theme of Indian love songs is parting. The Chippewa song given on page 74 may be regarded as an unusually fine example. In the old days it was the custom for Chippewa women to accompany their warriors a short distance from the village, all singing this song. As they turned back they continued their singing, which from the village could be heard at first faintly, then more plainly, as the women came sadly home to resume their tasks in loneliness.

Planning a raid at Wounded
Knee Creek, Teton Sioux.

Clear the Way

TETON SIOUX

Sung by Bear Eagle, about 1912

hã - ta yo_____ wa - kã - yã hi - bu we - lo e_____ o hã - ta_____
Clear the way! In a sa-cred man - ner I come, eh oh. Clear the

_____ yo wa - kã - yã hi - bu we - lo e_____ ma - ka
way!_____ In a sa-cred man - ner I come, eh._____ The

kĩ mi - ta - wa_____ cha wa - kã - yã hi - bu we - lo e_____ hã - ta
earth is mine._____ In a sa-cred man - ner I come, eh._____ Clear the

_____ yo_____ wa - kã - yã hi - bu we - lo e_____ yo
way!_____ In a sa - cred man - ner I come, eh yo.

hãta yo: clear the way | *wakãyã*: in a sacred manner | *hibu welo*: I come | *e,o*: meaningless | *maka kĩ*: the earth | *mita wa*: (is) mine | *cha*: therefore

Farewell to the Warriors

CHIPPEWA

Moderately slow (♩ = 76)

Sung by Mrs. Charles Mee, about 1908

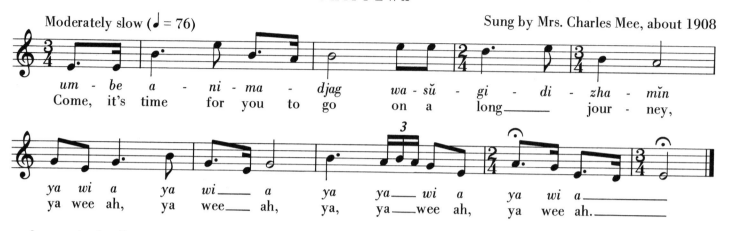

um - be a - ni - ma - djag   wa - sŭ - gi - di - zha - mĭn
Come, it's time for you to go   on a   long____ jour - ney,

ya   wi   a   ya   wi____ a   ya   ya____ wi   a   ya   wi   a____
ya   wee   ah,   ya   wee____ ah,   ya,   ya____wee   ah,   ya   wee   ah.____

umbe: come | *animadjag*: it is time for you to depart | *wasŭgidizhamĭn*: we are going on a long journey | *ya wi a etc.*: meaningless

This brief melody is of a type that enchanted the romantically minded European and American composers of the period 1900-1920, resulting in now forgotten pieces by Edward MacDowell, Rudolph Friml, Charles Wakefield Cadman, and others.

Remembering Brave Deeds

Songs of bravery would naturally be sung at the victory dance following a successful battle. On such an occasion war songs of past years and of heroes long dead might also be heard. And these, moreover, might be sung at any tribal gathering, not necessarily a victory celebration.

The song given on page 76 is unusual in that it recalls

the bravery of a woman, the Chippewa heroine Bicáganab, who defended her people during a surprise attack by Sioux raiders. Frances Densmore, who collected the song, records the following story of that event.

"One day as Bicáganab was lighting her breakfast fire, she heard the cry, 'The Sioux are upon us!' This was followed by the sound of gunfire. Immediately the camp became a scene of confusion, the men trying to drive off the Sioux and the women hurrying to put their household goods into canoes.

"The father of Bicáganab, who had joined the fight, was wounded five times but managed to get near enough to the water to be helped into a canoe. It was believed that Bicáganab had been killed.

"But when the people who had escaped in canoes were far from shore, they saw a woman fighting the Sioux with a club. The Sioux drove her into the water, and she swam toward a canoe. The Sioux followed, trying to club her, but she actually broke and tore their canoe with her hands. It was said that she was like a great bear in her ferocity. The Sioux were forced into the water and she pounded them with a paddle as they made for shore.

Odjibway, Chippewa warrior and singer.

Song for a Woman Who Was Brave in War

Sung by Odjibway, about 1908

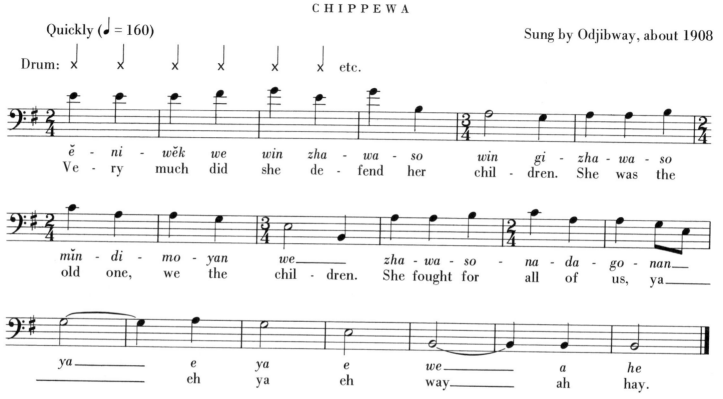

ĕniwĕk: very much | we: meaningless | win: she | [gi-]zhawaso: defending her children | mĭndimoyan: the old one (female) ([gigi-]
zhawasonadagonan: fought for us all | ya e we a he: meaningless

76

"Instead of following the retreating Chippewa, she went upstream, hiding in the bushes, returning later to the scene of battle by a roundabout path. There she found the Sioux that had been killed, covered with blankets. Beside them lay their guns and much beautiful beadwork. Bicáganab scalped the Sioux, put on a Sioux war bonnet, and made a great pack of blankets, guns, and beadwork. Then she painted her face and went back to the Chippewa camp with her trophies."

Flute Lure

Evening has arrived, and as the young girl busies herself with her sewing or beadwork she hears the call of a distant flute. "Mother," she says, "I must go to the stream for water." And the mother, allowing herself to be deceived, tells the girl she may go—provided she brings along her sister, however.

In the tall grasses beside the stream the girl will meet the boy whose flute call she has recognized. Perhaps the sister's boyfriend will be there too, and here at a safe distance from the lodges there will be a few moments for the talking and joking that are essential to courtship.

Such scenes were formerly common throughout the Plains and in the Eastern Woodlands. Flutes were also used for courting by young men in the Southwest and in other areas as well. The Indian lover's flute, however, was almost always a flageolet, meaning a flute with a whistle mouthpiece.

Love Signals

The Omaha love call on the opposite page is a typical young man's signal to his sweetheart. It says, in effect, "Come meet me by the stream." But more than this, it reveals the player's identity. Each young man has his own melody. The girl who hears it knows whose it is and whether or not it is meant for her.

In modern times young men of the Mexican Kickapoo tribe have fallen back on an alternate means of signaling that does not depend upon the flute. The Kickapoo, who formerly lived in Wisconsin and who moved in the nineteenth century to Mexico and to Oklahoma, have maintained their language and many of their Eastern Woodlands customs, more so in Mexico than in Oklahoma. Yet in Mexico the Kickapoo have lost the use of the flute. Instead, young men signal to their sweethearts by whistling into their hands (see picture on the next page).

Kickapoo courtship whistling follows the rhythms and accents of Kickapoo speech and can actually be used as a simple language. Typically a young man, perhaps joined by several companions, builds a fire not far from the village. At dark and throughout the evening one or more of the boys can be heard signaling: "Come on!" or

"What's keeping you?" The girls also know the whistling technique and answer: "No!" or "I'm thinking of you" or "I'm coming."

Beside the fire the young people sing and drink until as late as midnight. Although at least some of the parents object to this practice, they are apparently unable to put an end to it.

Courtship whistling has also been reported among the Flathead Indians of Montana, and no doubt other tribes have used it as well. It is for signaling only. But flute playing itself may be used either as a signal or as a serenade.

Love Call

OMAHA

Anonymous, about 1900

Courtship whistling, Kickapoo.

Signaling with the flute, Omaha.

Love Magic

Many of the Indian flute calls that have been recorded sound rather cheerful to the modern ear. There are others, however, that can only be regarded as mournful.

Often a lover will sing, rather than play, his love song, and songs of this sort are typically sad, expressing the lover's loneliness. Or in some cases, such songs may be addressed to a young woman for the purpose of making

Lonesome Flute

YUCHI

Played by Jim Tiger, about 1900

Moderato (♩ = 84)

repeat ad lib.
with variations

Flute Song

PIMA

Anonymous, 1927

Rapidly (♩ = 124)

ku - nye - ya ku - hu - na_____ che - yu - wĕ wa - ĕ - mwe - ta - ka
I play my flute and shake___ her heart.___ I play my___ flute and

yung - a - nye - na_____ ta - sha - ĕ wa - i - ni kĕ - ma___ kĕ - na ka -
shake__ her heart.___ Oh, when the sun__ goes down,___ I make my

e - pwĕ - ta che - yo - se - no ka - yung - a - nye - na___
flo - wers___ bloom,_____ I shake__ her heart.___

from the beginning

kunyeya kuhuna cheyuwĕ waĕmweta kayunganyena: I am playing (the flute) here, am shaking the woman's heart | *tashaĕ waini*
kĕma: when the sun goes down | *kĕna kaepwĕta cheyoseno*: I am making (flowers) bloom | *kayunganyena*: I am shaking her heart

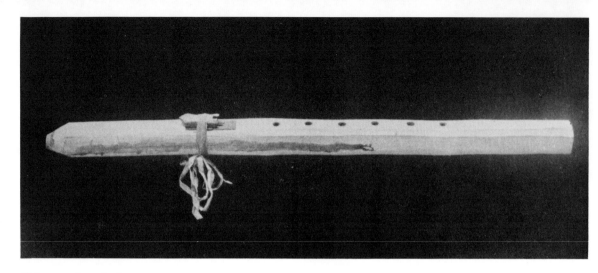

Chippewa lover's flute.

her feel lonely. If the magic is strong enough, she will be drawn irresistibly into his arms.

Penobscot love songs used to be called "songs of loneliness." Among the Kwakiutl, love songs and mourning songs were known by a single name. These Kwakiutl songs openly imitated crying and were sometimes sung in falsetto, usually with a vibrating tone.

The Yuchi flute melody on page 81 was played by a man who, when he had finished, exclaimed, "Oh, if some girls were only here! When they hear that, they cry, and then you can fondle them. It makes them feel lonesome. I wish some were here now. I feel badly myself."

But not all love magic is intended to induce loneliness. Sometimes the desired effect is a trance. In the Pima song given on page 81 the singer speaks of "shaking" the woman's heart as he makes his song "bloom." This music, although it is sung, imitates the sound of the Pima flute and has a decidedly hypnotic quality.

I Have Found My Lover

CHIPPEWA

Sung by Julia Warren Spears, 1908

nya: Oh! (woman's exclamation of surprise) | *nindinĕndŭm*: I am thinking | *mekawianin*: I have found | *ninimushĕn*: my lover | *sa*: meaningless

It should be pointed out that the Pima flute (actually a flageolet) has only three holes and thus a very limited range. The notes are low and plaintive.

Women's Love Songs

Indian women do not play the flute. Yet they have as many love songs as the men, many of which are songs of farewell or loneliness. Among the most beautiful are those recorded by Frances Densmore in the early 1900s in Chippewa country. A typically poignant Chippewa love song, recorded by Densmore, is given on page 74.

On this page is an unusually cheerful one. This song, like all Chippewa love songs, should be sung with a squawking nasal tone in imitation of the flageolet.

Songs for the Dead

At the death of an important member of the Omaha tribe, young men selected as official mourners would slit the flesh of their left arms and insert willow twigs. As they stood bleeding before the relatives of the deceased, singing the tribal song for the dead, the relatives would thank them for their sympathy. But the words to the song itself had quite a different purpose: they were addressed to the spirit of the dead person, urging it to go gladly on its way.

This emphasis upon mourning, on one hand, combined with the need to get rid of the ghost, on the other hand, is typical of native funerals on the Plains and in the Southwest. On the southern plains and in the Pueblo area the fear of the ghost becomes dominant. Among the Navajo this fear is so intense that funerals are carried out simply and quickly, or even avoided wherever possible.

But in the East and in the Far West we find elaborate tribal ceremonies for the dead in which the fear expressed in the central area is reversed and becomes a fascination.

In the East

Perhaps the most famous native American funerary ritual is the so-called Feast of the Dead, formerly celebrated by the Hurons and their closely related neighbors, the Iroquois. Among the Hurons, as we know from the seventeenth-century reports of Jesuit missionaries, this ritual was held only after the passage of about twelve years, at which time the corpses of all who had died since the last Feast would be exhumed from their temporary burials and the remaining flesh lovingly removed by women relatives.

When the bones had been cleaned and washed, they were wrapped in fine furs and carried to a central village, where people from all parts of the Huron world had gathered with similar bundles. The bundles were then "entertained" with music, feasting, and athletic games. Finally they were emptied into a huge pit and sealed over with logs, and the valuable furs were distributed as gifts to the living.

Common graves are no longer used, but to this day there are Iroquois groups that honor their loved ones in an annual *Ohgiwe,* or Dead Feast, at which time special *Ohgiwe* songs are sung.

In the Far West

Funerals on a grand scale were typical of the peoples who lived on or near the Pacific coast. In southern California the Diegueño, Yuma, and other tribes held a Mourning Anniversary every few years in which near-life-sized images of the dead were displayed and people attempted to outdo each other in their outpourings of grief.

Along the Bering Strait, Alaskan Eskimos held an annual Inviting-in Feast, to which they summoned the souls of all the recently dead. The "guests" were invited by pounding on the floor of the lodge, which caused the souls to leave their graves and move underground to a point directly below the fireplace. Then each person who had lost a relative would sing a mourning song to his loved one. A man might sing:

> O, my brother, come back to me,
> Come back, my brother, I am lonely.

But the best-known mourning ceremonies among the western Indians are the so-called potlatches held by the Tlingit, the Tsimshian, and other Northwest Coast tribes. A potlatch is a ritual in which valuable property is given away by a rich man in order to prove his importance and

Mourning Song for a Chief

TSIMSHIAN

Moderato (♩ = 78)

Sung by Alfred Skateen, about 1925

no   ha - no   e   hi_____   hi_____   ye_____   ye_____

hano: meaningless word used in Northwest Coast mourning songs | *hi ye etc.*: meaningless | *takòk*: the first, or the head (chief) | *suwóde*: they call him

lay claim to a high title. Among the Tlingit and the Tsimshian, potlatches are almost exclusively used for the purpose of mourning a dead chief—and establishing the authority of his successor. People from all over, and sometimes even people from foreign tribes, are invited to an important potlatch. Lavish gifts of blankets, furs, food, and ornaments are given away by the new chief in thanks to those who have come to help him mourn.

This might also be the occasion for other members of the tribe to renew their claims to particular titles or privileges. Any important man might display his crown, or "crest," to the gathered crowd, give away gifts, and have a singer perform the mourning song associated with the crest, a song in memory of the ancestor from whom the title is descended. Crests, stacked one on top of another, comprise the so-called totem poles, several of which are shown in the picture on page 37.

Tsimshian and Tlingit mourning songs are therefore used for a practical purpose, often years or even generations removed from the actual death of the person commemorated. It might be supposed that such songs would arouse little if any emotion. Yet just the opposite is true. Even when performing into the recording machine of an anthropologist, Tsimshian and Tlingit singers have been known to break into sobs, at times uncontrollably.

The picture of John Lakneets on page 88 shows the proper manner of singing Tsimshian mourning songs with a hand drum. The other picture on page 88 shows the Lakneets grave house, a typical and ancient form of Northwest Coast burial, even though in this case the materials with which the tomb is constructed are modern.

The Tlingit mourning song on page 89 is said to have been composed in the remote past by a man who accidentally shot and killed his brother. Though composed in

John Lakneets, Tsimshian singer.

Lakneets family grave house,
Kitwanga, British Columbia.

Mourning Song for a Brother

TLINGIT

Sung by Maggie Harry and
Jenny Jack, 1954

'adjushi kine 'aya: my little brother | shikayeya: where are you? | mayu: why did I do it? | matai 'a:? | nitle 'a: come back to me(?) |
(Note: These words are not in Tlingit but in the language of the neighboring Ahtena tribe, where the song is believed to have
originated.)

Tsimshian potlatch, Port Simpson,
British Columbia.

the language of the Ahtena, a tribe farther inland and
to the north, the song has been used in recent years by
the Tlingit family-group called Kwashkwan. At a potlatch it is sung by all members of the group, both men
and women, swaying back and forth as they sing. The
men sing bass and tenor, while the women sing alto and
soprano, making a choir in four octaves (without har-
mony). The singers are accompanied by a drummer.

Singing for a New Life

Many of the songs in this book, or songs like them, are still being sung today. By keeping alive the old songs and dances, Indians remain in touch with their cultural heritage. Musical performances are a regular feature of the modern Indian gatherings, or fairs, usually called pow-wows, held in Oklahoma and in many other regions as well.

But mere showmanship does not satisfy the need for a better life. Indian groups still keenly feel the loss of tribal lands and the natural wealth that was once theirs. Like other conquered peoples throughout the history of the world, American Indians have attempted to make up for their losses by devising new forms of political and religious expression commonly referred to by anthropologists as "revitalization movements."

The best-known Indian revitalization movements are the Ghost Dance of the late nineteenth century and the modern Peyote religion. Music was, or is, a prominent feature of both.

The Ghost Dance

In the 1870s and 1880s, as white settlers poured westward, the great herds of game animals that had been the Indians' main source of food began to diminish rapidly. During these years there arose a number of Indian religious leaders preaching special rituals to get rid of the whites and bring back the vanished animals.

The most famous of these prophets was the mystical

Dancing at a modern powwow in
South Dakota.

Arapaho Ghost Dance singers.

Wovoka, also known as Jack Wilson, a Paiute of northern Nevada. In 1886 Wovoka reported a vision, or prophecy, in which the earth was covered over by a rolling mass of mud and water, destroying all the whites and everything they had brought with them. In order to escape destruction the Indians were told to dance the round dance, and as they danced, the flood would pass under them. When it was over, the earth would turn green again, the animals would reappear, and all the ancestral dead, or ghosts, would come back to life.

The dancing began in Nevada and spread eastward from tribe to tribe until by 1890 it had reached the Co-

92

manche, the Arapaho, the Sioux, and others. It was believed that the dancing would hasten the fulfillment of the prophecy.

Wovoka preached that the dance should last five days and be held at least once a month. Both men and women danced, holding hands in a circle, shuffling leftward as they sang songs in which each phrase was repeated once before going on to the next phrase. This kind of repetition is unusual in Indian music and is an essential feature of Ghost Dance singing. In most tribes the songs were sung in unison by the dancers without any accompaniment. The fact that men and women danced together is also unusual and, in this case, shows modern influence.

As the dance progressed, it would get gradually faster. People would begin to feel the hypnotic power of the music. Perhaps a woman would begin to tremble. Then a medicine man, who had been standing in the center of the circle waiting for this sign, would come over and dance in front of the woman, twirling a feather before her face. Partially hypnotized she would stagger out from

Father, Have Pity on Me
ARAPAHO GHOST DANCE

Anonymous, 1894

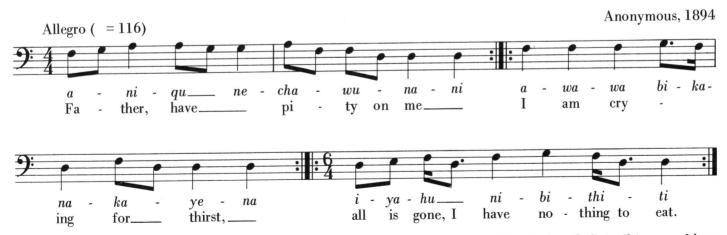

aniqu nechawunani: Father, have pity on me | *awawa bikanakayena*: I am crying for thirst | *iyahu nibithiti*: all is gone—I have nothing to eat

Yellow Light from Sun Is Streaming

COMANCHE GHOST DANCE

Moderato (♩ = 84)

Anonymous, 1894

he - yo he - yo - ha - na ha - e - yo he - yo - ha - na ha - e - yo
Hay - yo! Hay - yo 'ha - na ha - eh - yo! Hay - yo ha - na ha - eh - yo!

Faster (♩ = 120)

te - a - ya to - ra - bi ai - gi - na he e yo
Light from sun is flow - ing,___ hay eh yo!

te - a - ya to - a - ha ta - bi won - gi - na hi hi yo
Yel - low light from sun___ is___ stream - ing,___ hee hee yo!

he-e-yo etc.: meaningless | *teaya torabi aigina*: the sun's beams are running out | *teaya toaha tabi wongin*: the sun's yellow rays are running out

the circle, the medicine man continuing to hold her under his influence, until she finally fell to the ground in a trance.

Minutes or hours later, when the woman returned to her senses, she would be brought to the center of the circle to report her experiences in the other world, where invariably she would have met the ghost of a departed friend or relative, who perhaps had taught her a song. In this way new Ghost Dance songs were composed, or revealed.

The teachings of Wovoka were outwardly peaceful. He emphasized that the new world would come into being as a result of the dance itself, without the need for armed resistance. Nevertheless, as the Ghost Dance spread, whites became alarmed. In Sioux country, especially, it was believed that the Indians were on the verge of an outbreak. The episode came to a climax at Wounded Knee, South Dakota, in the notorious massacre of December 29, 1890, in which two hundred mostly unarmed Indian men, women, and children were killed by U.S. Army gunfire.

After Wounded Knee, the Ghost Dance began to die out. It was replaced by a much quieter religion, which taught personal salvation through the eating of peyote.

The Peyote Religion

Peyote is a spineless member of the cactus family, native to southern Texas and Mexico. It grows close to the ground forming small pincushionlike mounds, or "buttons." If you pronounce it PAY-oat, it will sound almost like the original Aztec name, *peyotl,* actually pronounced PAY-ootl, with the final *tl* like the *tl* in the English word *atlas.* Today most people pronounce it more or less in the Spanish way: pay-YO-dy (rhymes with Hey, Jody).

Indian people from as far away as southern Canada regularly travel to Texas or Mexico in order to bring home a load of peyote buttons for their religious ceremonies. The typical ritual starts in the evening after dark and lasts until daybreak. The participants sit in a circle, often in a tepee, and sing Peyote songs until midnight or later, when special prayers are offered. Then the singing is usually resumed. Each person in turn sings one or more songs to the accompaniment of a water drum and often a rattle as well.

Peyote songs are brisk in tempo, accompanied by the rapid, steady beat of the drum. Some of the songs have words, but meaningless syllables are typical. The song given on page 97 is an unusually fine example. It was collected among the Delawares of Oklahoma, where the Peyote religion is especially strong.

Oklahoma Peyote drummer.

As the songs drone on, the participant, who may have eaten a large number of peyote buttons, will begin to feel the effects of the drug. If he is fortunate he will experience the psychedelic color-visions for which peyote, like LSD, is well known. Perhaps he will see an eagle, surrounded by kaleidoscopic colors, or a dead relative returned to life in a beautiful landscape.

For a modern Indian such hallucinations are equivalent to the visions sought in the old days through fasting (see page 45). These visions bring spiritual power, giving the Peyotist strength to face day-to-day problems, which may include a low-paying job, discrimination by whites, and the temptation to drink.

As in the Ghost Dance, there are unmistakable Christian elements in the Peyote religion. God the Father and Jesus Christ are frequently invoked in Peyote prayers. But the form of the ritual, as well as the music, is strictly Indian.

The Peyote religion today numbers perhaps as many as 250,000 adherents—both men and women—mostly on the Plains and in parts of the Southwest. As a revitalization movement it does not appear to have much po-

Peyote Song

DELAWARE

Sung by Charlton L. Wilson, about 1950

Modern Peyote ceremony,
Saskatchewan.

litical content. Yet whites have feared it, and attempts have been made to outlaw the use of peyote. To meet the challenge, Peyotists have organized themselves into an official group called the Native American Church, set up for the explicit purpose of heading off religious discrimination. In this they have been largely successful. Peyote, if used by members of the Church, is now legal in many (though not all) states.

Some of the songs used in the ritual are actually composed under the influence of peyote. Peyote songs are continually being created, amply demonstrating that Indian music, even today, is a living art capable of developing new songs and new styles.

Key to Musical Symbols

All musical symbols appearing in this book have the usual meanings. But the following points should be noted.

Bar lines are included to facilitate reading. They do not necessarily imply an accent on the first beat of each "measure" as in Western music.

Repeats, especially internal repeats, are not optional. They are necessary to the structure of the music.

The hold (⌒), appearing directly over a note, means that the sound should be prolonged about a quarter of its normal length in the case of a half note, less in the case of a whole note. If it appears over a space between notes it signals a short silence sufficient to allow the singer a fresh breath—not a gasp but a comfortable inhalation. The rhythmic accompaniment, if there is one, does not wait, however. It goes right on, falling out of synchronization with the melody, perhaps catching up later on.

The noise note (✗) is an impure sound: a drum or rattle beat, a shout, a howl, etc.

The headless noise note (✗⌐), written as the second of a pair with a regular noise note, signals the weak beat in rattling, the faint noise as the hand is lifted in preparation for the next downstroke.

The horizontal waved line (∿∿∿) denotes continuous rattling.

Key to Pronunciation

Unmarked vowels have the usual Spanish or Italian sounds: *a* as in *father*, *e* as the *a* in *plate*, *i* as the *ee* in *meet*, *o* as in *hope*, and *u* as the *oo* in *shoot*. You will also find *ao* (as the *ow* in *how*) and *ai* (as the *i* in *right*).

Nasal vowels are pronounced in the same way, except that the nasal passages must be closed, giving the sound a kind of grunting tone. Nasals are common in French but are never used in formal English. When you say *unh-unh* (meaning "no"), or when you go *oonh!* (as you strain to push open a stuck door), you are uttering a nasal sound. Nasals are written thus: *ã, ĩ*, etc.

Other marked vowels are as follows: *ă* as in *hat*, *ĕ* as in *met*, *ĭ* as in *hit*, *ŭ* as in *but*, *ŏŏ* as in *book*, *ȯ* as the *aw* in *law*.

Consonant and consonant combinations are as in English. But *g* is always as in *get*; *th* as in *these*; *s* as in *sofa*; *ng* as in *young* (not as in *anger*); *q* marks a *k* sound pronounced so deep in the throat that it sounds like a rasping *ch* or a dry gargle; *kw* at the end of a syllable is pronounced like a *k* but with the lips pursed as though pronouncing a *w*. Unusual consonant pairs (like *tl*, *pw*, or *mw*) can be correctly guessed by simply combining the normal English sounds of the separate letters.

The apostrophe (') signals a glottal stop, a catch in the throat, frequent in English conversation but never written. When you say *unh-unh* (meaning "no") you are really saying *'unh-'unh*. If you are very precise, you will put on your *mit-tens*, but most people probably say *mit'ens*. Glottal stops are more important in Indian languages than they are in English.

Suggestions for Further Reading

Curtis, Natalie. *The Indians' Book: Songs and Legends of the American Indians,* 1907, 2d ed. 1923; reprint of 2d ed. by Dover Publications, 1968. Includes accurate transcriptions (with Indian words and English translations) of 150 songs from the Penobscot, Sioux, Pawnee, Cheyenne, Arapaho, Kiowa, Winnebago, Navajo, Zuni, Hopi, Kwakiutl, and other tribes. The accompanying commentary is rich in content if old-fashioned in style.

The works of Frances Densmore. Densmore was by far the most prolific collector of Indian songs. Her earliest collections are her best: *Chippewa Music,* 2 vols., 1910 and 1913, reprinted in 1 vol. by Ross and Haines, 1973; and *Teton Sioux Music,* 1918, reprinted by Da Capo Press, 1972. Her later collections —of Pawnee, Cheyenne, Santo Domingo, Papago, Yaqui and Yuman, Nootka and Quileute, Seminole, Choctaw, Menominee, Northern Ute, Mandan and Hidatsa, and Pueblo music —are useful but do not as a rule include the original words to the songs.

The works of Gertrude P. Kurath. Kurath is the only student of Indian dance music who has accurately recorded the steps that go with the songs. Two of her fullest works are *Iroquois Music and Dance,* 1964, reprinted by Scholarly Press; and *Music and Dance of the Tewa Pueblos,* Museum of New Mexico press, 1970.

Nettl, Bruno. *Music in Primitive Culture,* Harvard, 1956. Ethnomusicology for the general reader, with emphasis on American Indian songs. Serious students will also consult Nettl's *North American Indian Styles,* Memoirs of the American Folklore Society, vol. 45, 1954, and his *Reference Materials in Ethnomusicology: A Bibliographic Essay,* 2d rev. ed., Information Coordinators, Inc., Detroit, 1967.

Suggestions for Listening

Listening to Indian music is not something that should be entered into lightly. The native performer's mannerisms and tonal quality may at first seem so strange that the music itself will be missed entirely. It would be far better to learn one or two songs from the transcriptions in this book, then try listening to the actual performance on the companion album, *A Cry From the Earth*. Once you've gained a little experience you should try one or more songs by listening to the performance first. And this of course is the way Indian singers themselves learn new pieces. The asterisks on pages 112-113 will show you which of the songs in this book can be heard on the Folkways album.

The companion phonograph album, originally Folkways Records FC 7777, is now number 3777 in the Folkways Cassette Series. It is available from:

Folkways
Office of Folklife Programs
955 L'Enfant Plaza 2600
Smithsonian Institution
Washington, D.C. 20560
Price: $10.95 please include shipping

Selected Text References

page 3 / Navajo "cover": G. Reichard, *Navaho Religion*, 288. *page 5* / old-time Ute: F. Densmore, *Northern Ute Music*, 26, 62. *page 6* / speech rhythm: cf. Curt Sachs, *Rhythm and Tempo: A Study in Music History*, 21–38. *page 6* / music comes from dance: Ezra Pound, *ABC of Reading*. *page 11* / Navajo tones: G. Herzog, "Speech Melody..." in *Musical Quarterly*, vol. 20, 452–66. *page 11* / Spencer's theory: ibid. *page 12* / earth mother: Reichard, op. cit., 284. *page 13* / serpent myth: Edw. Curtis, *The North American Indian*, vol. 15, 121. *page 13* / groups corresponding to geographical areas: For the treatment of this subject, including the names given the various areas, I am indebted to the writings of George Herzog and Helen Roberts and, especially, to Bruno Nettl's *North American Indian Musical Styles*. *page 18* / swallows a piece of turquoise: David MacAllester, *Enemy Way Music*, 73. *page 27* / stone gongs and the tendency to shift the pitch: F. Densmore, *Music of Santo Domingo Pueblo*, 45, 53. *page 28* / included with eastern Asia: B. Nettl, *Music in Primitive Culture*, 142; see also Nettl's *Folk and Traditional Music of the Western Continents*, 148. *page 32* / Crow lullabies: R. Lowie, *The Crow Indians*. *page 32* / horned toad: F. Densmore, *Music of Acoma, Isleta, Cochiti, and Zuñi*. *page 36* / "I am your slave" or "I am your dog": paraphrased after F. Boas, *Kwakiutl Ethnography* (Univ. of Chicago, 1966), 346. *page 44* / Red Weasel: F. Densmore, *Teton Sioux Music*, 88. *page 55* / group dances . . . solo dances: G. Kurath, "Native Choreographic Areas of North America" in *American Anthropologist*, vol. 55 (1953), 60–73; see also Kurath's "American Indian Peoples, Arts of: Dance" in *New Encyclopaedia Britannica*, 15th ed., *Macropaedia*, vol. 1, 669–76. *page 79* / Kickapoo whistling: R. E. Ritzenthaler and F. A. Peterson, *The Mexican Kickapoo Indians*. *page 84* / Huron Feast of the Dead: B. Trigger, *The Huron*. *page 85* / Mourning Anniversary and Inviting-in Feast: R. Underhill, *Red Man's Religion*.

Sources for the Songs

Note / Many of these songs have been transposed one or two halftones higher (or lower) in order to avoid difficult key signatures. In any event it is often impossible to determine the original pitch with complete accuracy, especially in the case of older recordings.

page 17 / Reproduced after J.F. de Galaup, Comte de La Pérouse, in Frederica de Laguna, *Under Mt. St. Elias: The History and Culture of the Yakutat Tlingit*, Smithsonian Contributions to Anthropology, vol. 7, pt. 2, 1972, p. 560.

page 21 / Transcribed from Willard Rhodes, *Indian Songs of Today*, Library of Congress phonograph disc AFS L36.

page 29 / Natalie Curtis, *The Indians' Book*, Harper and Brothers, 2d ed., 1923, p. 529. Copyright © renewed 1950 by Paul Burlin. Quoted by permission of Barbara B. Wedell.

page 33 / Transcribed from Willard Rhodes, *Folk Music of the United States: Pueblo*, Library of Congress phonograph disc

AFS L43, side B, band 5. As recorded, the song is sung three times: the first time has measure 3 omitted; the second time is straight through as written; the third time has only measures 3, 2, 4, and the first four beats of 5, in that order. For the title and the translation of the Hopi words I am indebted to Frederick J. Dockstader and to the similar, but not identical, version of this song transcribed in Natalie Curtis, op. cit., pp. 498, 558.

page 34 / Transcribed from Willard Rhodes, *Folk Music of the United States: Delaware, Cherokee, Choctaw, Creek*, Library of Congress phonograph disc AFS L37, side A, band 4. For the translation of the words I am indebted to Duane H. King, Director of the Museum of the Cherokee Indian, Cherokee, N.C.

page 36 / Natalie Curtis, *The Indians' Book*, Harper and Brothers, 2d ed., 1923, pp. 303, 307. Copyright © renewed 1950 by Paul Burlin. Quoted by permission of Barbara B. Wedell.

page 38 / Marius Barbeau, "Tsimshian Songs," in Viola E. Garfield, Paul S. Wingert, and Marius Barbeau, *The Tsimshian: Their Arts and Music*, Publications of the American Ethnological Society, XVIII, 1951, song no. 56. Transposed about an octave and a half higher.

page 42 / Transcribed from J.P. Harrington Picuris collection, No. 5, Archive of Folk Song, Library of Congress. Compare J. P. Harrington and Helen H. Roberts, "Picurís Children's Stories," *43rd Annual Report of the Bureau of American Ethnology, 1925–26*, 1928, pp. 339–343.

page 45 / Alice C. Fletcher and Francis La Flesche, "The Omaha Tribe," *27th Annual Report of the Bureau of American Ethnology, 1905–1906*, 1911, p. 130.

page 47 / Transcribed from Indiana University Archives of Traditional Music Acc. No. 57-014-F (Atl 1462.11), Edward S. Curtis Nez Percé collection. Compare Edward S. Curtis, *The North American Indian*, vol. 8, 1911, p. 58.

page 49 / Transcribed from William N. Fenton, *Songs From the Iroquois Longhouse*, Library of Congress phonograph disc AFS L6, side A, band 8.

page 51 / Transcribed from Diamond Jenness collection, 1915–1916, no. IV-C-83 (78a), courtesy of Canadian Ethnology Service, National Museums of Canada. Compare Helen H. Roberts and D. Jenness, *Songs of the Copper Eskimo*, 1925, pp. 334, 492. The English words fitted to the music are those of C. M. Bowra, from his *Primitive Song*, World Publishing Co., 1962, p. 62.

page 53 / Washington Matthews, *Navajo Legends*, 1897, p. 258. Also see Matthews' "Navajo Gambling Songs," *American Anthropologist*, vol. 2, 1889, p. 19.

page 57 / George Herzog, "The Yuman Musical Style," *Journal of American Folklore*, vol. 41, 1928, p. 217. Rattle notation reconstructed from ibid., pp. 191 and 195.

page 59 / Wallace L. Chafe, *Seneca Thanksgiving Rituals*, Bureau of American Ethnology, Bulletin 183, 1961, pp. 2 (n. 3), 61–2, 301. For the dance steps see Gertrude P. Kurath, *Iroquois Music and Dance*, Bureau of American Ethnology, Bulletin 187, 1964, pp. 5, 53, 57, 93, 99, 198.

page 64 / Transcribed from Willard Rhodes, *Folk Music of the United States: Navaho*, Library of Congress phonograph disc AFS L41, side A, band 1.

page 67 / Transcribed from Indiana University Archives of Traditional Music Acc. No. 57-014-F (Atl 1462.11), Edward Speck Penobscot collection, courtesy of University of Pennsylvania Museum. Compare Frank G. Speck, *Penobscot Man*, University of Pennsylvania, 1940, pp. 170 and 280.

page 68 / Frances Densmore, "Choctaw Music," *Anthropological Papers 27–32*, Bureau of American Ethnology, Bulletin 136, 1943, p. 176.

page 73 / ———, *Teton Sioux Music*, Bureau of American Ethnology, Bulletin 61, 1918, p. 351.

page 74 / ———, *Chippewa Music*, Bureau of American Ethnology, Bulletin 45, 1910, p. 163.

page 76 / ———, *Chippewa Music II*, Bureau of American Ethnology, Bulletin 53, 1913, p. 131.

page 79 / Alice C. Fletcher and Francis La Flesche, op. cit., p. 319. An adaptation for piano and voice appears as No. 3 in Charles Wakefield Cadman, *Four American Indian Songs* (Op. 45), White-Smith Music Publishing Co., Boston, 1909, p. 16.

page 81, top / Transcribed from Indiana University Archives of Traditional Music Acc. No. Pre '54-141-F (Atl 1946.2), Frank G. Speck Yuchi collection, courtesy of American Museum of Natural History. Compare Frank G. Speck, *Ethnology of the Yuchi Indians*, Anthropological Publications of the University Museum, University of Pennsylvania, vol. 1, no. 1, 1909, p. 63.

page 81, bottom / George Herzog, "A Comparison of Pueblo and Pima Musical Styles," *Journal of American Folklore*, vol. 49, 1936, pp. 331, 395.

page 83 / Frances Densmore, *Chippewa Music II*, Bureau of American Ethnology, Bulletin 53, 1913, p. 300.

page 86 / Marius Barbeau, op. cit., song no. 69. The melody for the second verse is sung with slight variations not noted here. Transposed about an octave higher.

page 89 / Transcribed from Archive of Folk Song 11,937A3, LWO 3707R4 (Library of Congress). The repeats are taken with variations not noted here. Compare de Laguna, op. cit., pt. 3, pp. 1156, 1183.

page 93 / Transcribed from Archive of Folk Song 14,041B (Library of Congress). Compare James Mooney, "The Ghost-Dance Religion," *14th Annual Report of the Bureau of American Ethnology, 1892–93, 1896*, Arapaho song no. 28.

page 94 / Transcribed from Archive of Folk Song 14,035A (Library of Congress). Compare James Mooney, op. cit., Comanche song no. 1.

page 97 / Transcribed from Willard Rhodes, *Folk Music of the United States: Delaware, Cherokee, Choctaw, Creek*, Library of Congress phonograph disc AFS L37, side A, band 2, song 3.

Sources for the Pictures

page 4 / Edward S. Curtis, *The North American Indian*, supplement to vol. 10, Pl. 355. Courtesy of Vassar College.

page 7 / Smithsonian Institution, neg. NAA 1101-B-2.

page 9 / Edward S. Curtis, op. cit., supplement to vol. 5, Pl. 161. Courtesy of Vassar College.

page 10 / Museum of New Mexico, neg. 42311 (photo by J.R. Willis).

page 11 / Edward S. Curtis, op. cit., vol. 16, p. 10. Courtesy of Vassar College.

page 16 / University of Alaska Archives, accession 73-66-55.

page 19 / Museum of New Mexico, neg. 3038 (photo by T. Harmon Parkhurst).

page 22 / National Film Board of Canada, neg. 100365. Courtesy of Canadian Consulate General, New York.

page 25 / Frances Densmore, *Chippewa Music*, Pl. 1.

page 27 / Author's collection.

page 28 / Museum of the American Indian, Heye Foundation, neg. 37925.

page 30, left / Edward S. Curtis, op. cit., supplement to vol. 18, Pl. 623. Courtesy of Vassar College.

page 30, right / National Museums of Canada, neg. 78657.

page 35 / Edward S. Curtis, op. cit., vol. 4, p. 178. Courtesy of Vassar College.

page 37 / National Museums of Canada, neg. 62440.

page 41 / Smithsonian Institution, neg. NAA 2073.

page 48 / Edward S. Curtis, op. cit., supplement to vol. 18, Pl. 634. Courtesy of Vassar College.

page 49 / Author's collection.

page 50 / Photo RM 1580 from the collection of the Rochester Museum and Science Center, Rochester, N.Y.

page 51 / National Museums of Canada, neg. 50918.

page 52 / Smithsonian Institution, neg. 596-C-17.

page 58, left / Idem., neg. NAA 1102-B-30.

page 58, right / Accessions 70.89.30 and AE 347 from the collection of the Rochester Museum and Science Center, Rochester, N.Y.,

page 62 / Edward S. Curtis, op. cit., vol. 10. p. 276. Courtesy of Vassar College.

page 63 / Washington Matthews, *The Night Chant*, Pl. VII.

page 66 / National Aeronautics and Space Administration, neg. 77-H-508.

page 72 / Edward S. Curtis, op. cit., supplement to vol. 3, Pl. 98. Courtesy of Vassar College.

page 75 / Frances Densmore, *Chippewa Music II*, Pl. 1.

page 80, left / Smithsonian Institution, neg. 3987.

page 80, right / Milwaukee Public Museum, Milwaukee, Wisc., neg. 35-17:17.

page 82 / Frances Densmore, *Chippewa Music II*, Pl. 2.

page 88, left / National Museums of Canada, neg. 62478.

page 88, right / Idem., neg. 68456.

page 90 / Idem., neg. 47034.

page 92, left / Travel Division, South Dakota Department of Highways.

page 92, right / Smithsonian Institution, neg. NAA 55298.

page 96 / Edward S. Curtis, op. cit., supplement to vol. 19, Pl. 687. Courtesy of Vassar College.

page 98 / *Saskatoon Star-Phoenix*, 13 October 1956. Courtesy of Saskatchewan Archives Board.

Index to Songs by Musical Area and Tribe